The Silver Bullet

Fred Harrison

The Silver Bullet

Published in the UK in 2009 by
The International Union for Land Value Taxation
Studio 5, St. Oswald's Studio
Sedlescombe Road
London SW6 1RH
www.theIU.org

First published 2008

ISBN 978-0-904658-10-1

Text copyright © theIU 2008, 2009
The International Union for Land Value Taxation

Cover photo © Christian Misje/iStockPhoto
Typesetting and design by Heilbunth & Co

In Memoriam
This study is dedicated to the memory of Professor Dmitry Lvov. As Academician-Secretary of the Economics Department of the Russian Academy of Sciences, Doctor Lvov worked fearlessly to offer his people the antidote to shock therapy.

Acknowledgements
Assistance is gratefully acknowledged from Nicholas Dennys, Edward Dodson, Bryan Kavanagh and Irina Veselkova.
The author is responsible for any errors and for the views expressed in this study.

Contents

Prologue

Poverty: Redefining Rights & Obligations

History will not shine kindly on campaigners who disregard poverty's 'silver bullet'. The silver bullet does exist. The question is, can the thinking and political will be mobilised to erase the institutional foundations of poverty? The children of the world's 'bottom billion' expect of us nothing less.

Poverty is treated as the problem itself, rather than a symptom. That is why public policies will not eradicate it. Instead, poverty will continue to serve as the transmission mechanism for the profound crises that have converged into an epic global drama. Terrorism as a social process, climate change as the violent retribution of nature, the trading tensions between unbalanced economies—such manifestations of discontent may be traced back to injustices that affront humanity.

Poverty and inequality are increasing in both the rich nations of the West, and those that we shall designate as neo-colonised countries (see box over). But poverty is no more than one symptom of a set of social rules that are pathological in character. There is no technical reason why it should not be abolished. But those who exercise the most influence in the structures of power work diligently to avoid addressing root causes. Thanks to political pressure and humanitarian instincts, some of the worst excesses of poverty are alleviated for many people. But poverty is a common denominator of all societies and remains an institutionalised feature of the capitalist economy. It pervades the rich nations, camouflaged by the Welfare State.

The architects of the Welfare State were sincere in wishing to address deprivation in all its forms, but their approach—grounded in faulty doctrine—doomed the social experiment to ultimate failure.[1] In Britain, for example, government appropriates nearly half the national product with the ostensible purpose of equalising people's life chances. And yet, an estimated 27% of the population are classed as poor in the UK. Families that are not deemed to be impoverished because of transfers of other people's earnings can hardly be said to enjoy the dignified life of independent adults. Child poverty doubled in the 20 years to 1997.[2] With 3.8m British children living below the poverty line in 2007, the Conservative opposition launched a campaign to "Make British Poverty History".[3]

Poverty, both in the West and in the rest of the world, is an artificial construct. Its origins are rooted in a colonial history which will loom large in this study. By colonialism, we refer to that external intervention and control which had as its purpose the abuse of people's natural right of access to land and nature's resources. We will explain that consigning poverty to history will require the restitution of people's birthright in land.

Unravelling the injustices that sprang from colonialism will be achieved only by conjoining new approaches to land tenure and public finance. Given the modern methods for producing wealth, and the complexity of society in the 21st century, land reform

What's in a name?

LABELS used to designate non-Western countries are unsatisfactory. Concepts like Third World are now avoided. Similarly, 'developing' and 'less developed' concepts imply backwardness. Yet, these countries embarked on independence with their indigenous cultures degraded by the colonial experience: a legacy of property rights remains the primary obstacle to benign renewal.

The geographical designation—'the South'—is also anomalous. It conflates into a single category countries that are culturally diverse (some of which are in the northern hemisphere); and whose levels of income and cultural complexity are markedly different.

An accurate description for the former colonies of European powers is 'neo-colonised countries' (NCCs). Although now politically independent, the cultural and economic evolution of these sovereign nations is stunted by their retention of certain colonial laws and practices that serve powerful external interests. An example is India's Land Acquisition Act (1894), inherited from the British and used to grab land from farmers to build infrastructure like dams which, ultimately, have the effect of increasing the downstream value of assets owned by rich urban land owners.*

The reader will decide (as our analysis unfolds) whether the neo-colonised concept is analytically helpful in identifying remedies to deep-seated problems. Does China—which was not colonised—count as an NCC? Historian RH Tawney concurred with Dr. Sun Yat Sen's description of 19th century China as a colony, viewed from an economic point of view.** Furthermore, in the 20th century, China was blighted by a European import—the Marxist ideology.

Low income nations do need to change, and some are experimenting with new social models. They are re-developing, which acknowledges that long-standing barriers continue to obstruct cultural evolution in all of the countries that are the subject of this monograph. Their peoples have been denied the freedom to enjoy the living standards they would have chosen to earn for themselves.

* McDowell (1996) ** Tawney (1932) p. 129

cannot take the simple form of redistributing acres between the haves and the have-nots. Redistribution may be warranted, in some cases, but would not be sufficient to integrate economic efficiency with the principles of justice. The comprehensive restoration of people's right to land requires a reform of taxation—the crude pricing mechanism used to raise revenue for the public sector—in favour of charges for the use of land and nature's resources. We will explain in Part 3 that this delivers prosperity without the grievous deeds that created the environmental crisis and the separation of nations into rich and poor categories.

The administrative integration of land tenure with taxation, as the solution to poverty, is practical. The main challenge is the political will to consign poverty to history. But it would be a mistake to place all the blame on politicians. We also have to realise that there is a serious problem with the way eminent social scientists fail to come to terms with the existing knowledge base. We subject to close scrutiny the failings of one particularly influential scientist. Jeffrey Sachs bears the brunt of our interrogation because he has placed himself at the forefront of the global campaign against poverty, wearing the mantle of the United Nations to legitimise those policies which he favours. But it would not be fair to allow one man to carry all the responsibility. A short excursion into the history of economic ideas places our critique in its context.

Economics is a damaged social science because its exponents fail to work with comprehensive models of the real world. This failing is to be found on both the Left and the Right. Unfortunately, even those with the courage to challenge the power structure must share some of the responsibility for the failure to understand what needs to be done to solve problems like mass poverty (see box over). An example is provided by the case of Joseph Stiglitz, a Nobel Prize winner and former chief economist at the World Bank. He is a distinguished champion of the underdog. But one is obliged to inquire why he has fallen foul of the selective amnesia that curbs understanding of where the emphasis should be placed in the reform agenda.

Take Making Globalization Work, the latest work by Stiglitz. He identifies why the globalised economy malfunctions in a way that generates poverty. He correctly defines 'rent'—the value of the country's natural and common resources—and prescribes the remedial policy for poverty. The concept of rent will loom large in this monograph, particularly as it is used by academics.

> Bribery, cheating, and imbalanced negotiating all cut into what rightfully ought to go to the developing country. The countries get less than they should, the companies get more. A competitive market should mean that oil and mining companies simply get a normal return on their capital; excess returns should belong to the country owning the resources. Economists refer to the value of the resource in excess of the cost of extraction as natural resource 'rents.'[4]

We shall focus on the societal treatment of rent, because it is the lynchpin of any poverty elimination agenda. Understanding its nature and role in the market economy is a precondition for rebasing society on the principles of economic efficiency and of justice for everyone. Stiglitz knows this, and wants others to understand it. And yet, in his book, if you turn to the index, you will find nine listings for wages, six listings for profits, but not a single entry for rent. This omission is consistent with the failures of the post-classical school of economics as it is taught in universities. Having emphasised that poverty will not be abolished by continuing with present policies, we have to affirm that it is possible to abolish it. But reforms will not occur without an

Selective Amnesia in Social Science and Public Policy

NAOMI KLEIN is an eloquent champion of the poor. She uses her vitriolic pen to expose defects in the Chicago School brand of economics. In The Shock Doctrine: The Rise of Disaster Capitalism (2007) she attacks Professor Jeffrey Sachs as an acolyte of Milton Friedman, the economist vilified by the Left for the emphasis he placed on monetary policy and what Friedman promoted as free markets.

There is a problem with the Friedman model of economics. He failed to integrate into it the public policies that would optimise the efficiency and fairness of free markets and public services.

Friedman emphasised the need to shrink the size of government by cutting taxes. But the problem is not so much with how much revenue a government raises, as with how it raises revenue. Friedman did understand that this was the problem, so he ought to have emphasised the need to change tax policies.

As a scholar, he knew that taxes which damaged incentives to work, save and invest should be replaced with public charges on the rent of land in all its uses, and the rents which are paid for the use of the electromagnetic spectrum (which make mobile telephones possible) or for oil, diamonds and the rest of nature's freely given resources. He acknowledged, in an unguarded moment, that: "In my opinion the least bad tax is the property tax on the unimproved value of land, the Henry George argument of many, many years ago".*

But Friedman failed to instruct his students on the economics that would secure the outcome that was the best for everyone. So economists like Jeffrey Sachs voyaged forth into the world with an incomplete toolkit, the victim of selective amnesia.

But, likewise, ardent critics like Naomi Klein are silent on the model of economics that is compatible with good governance and justice.

* Harrison (1983) p. 299

informed debate on the causes of poverty, starting with this question: why do billions of people endure lives inferior to what they would choose for themselves? What represses their creative energy? Their cause is not best served by bypassing this question and going straight to slogans like Make Poverty History.

Our fundamental approach will be opposed by the vested interests, but we must persist. Our analytical framework reveals why the policies historically favoured by agencies such as the United Nations and the World Bank cannot succeed. The gatekeepers to our minds (the stewards of 'authorised discourse') do not want us to address the issue in radical terms, such as the proposition that poverty is the necessary consequence of the way we have written the rules that shape and regulate the market economy.

The scale of the problem that we address is awesome. The UN uses the World Bank's $1-a-day benchmark. According to the statistics, more than one billion people exist on a daily income of less than $1.[5] To address this blight on humanity, Kofi Annan, then General Secretary of the UN, threw down the gauntlet in 2000. One of the Millennium Development Goals was "halving the proportion of people living in extreme poverty, and so lifting more than 1bn people out of it, by 2015".[6] In setting its targets, the UN acknowledged that the gaps in income between the poorest and richest countries had widened in the last four decades of the 20th century.[7]

But according to research by World Bank economists and independent scholars, poverty has declined over the past 30 years. The table below offers four definitions of poverty. In each category, there have been significant improvements. Xavier Sala-i-Martin, a professor of economics at Columbia University, concludes, in relation to the UN Millennium Development Goal, that "when the goal was established in 2000, the world was already 60% of the way toward achieving it. The world might just be in better shape than many of our leaders believe".[8] But, as we shall see, this improvement is illusory.

No-one denies, however, that the scale of material deprivation remains so huge that it is beyond comprehension by those of us who enjoy what the philosopher Mortimer J Adler described as the goods necessary for a decent human existence.

Poverty Rates (%)							
Poverty line definition	1970	1975	1980	1985	1990	1995	2000
$1/day	15.4	14.0	11.9	8.8	7.3	6.2	5.7
$1.50/day	20.2	18.5	15.9	12.1	10.0	8.0	7.0
$2/day	29.6	27.5	24.2	19.3	16.2	12.6	10.6
$3/day	46.6	44.2	40.3	34.7	30.7	25.0	21.1

Source: Sala-i-Martin (2006) p. 121

- In the 20 years to the beginning of the new millennium, the percentage of the population of the neo-colonised world existing below $1-a-day was almost halved—but that left 1.1bn people in abject poverty.
- Even if current trends continue, World Bank economists project a poverty rate for 2015 that falls short of Millennium Development Goals, with 900m people living below $1-a-day, and a great many more just above that line.[9]

Hundreds of millions live on the edge of existence, and Professor Sala-i-Martin predicts that "unless the incomes of…African citizens begin to grow, and grow rapidly, world income inequality will start to rise again in a few years' time".[10]

If the number living on under $3-a-day has been declining, we shall see that this cannot be attributed to the UN or to Western aid donors. Nor has it been the result of strategies advocated by those who champion the combination of economic policies known as the Washington Consensus (see chapter 1).

Improvement in the numbers living in absolute poverty was the result, in the main, of heavily-populated nations turning away from state socialism. This is traced by the data in the table below, which summarises the numbers living on less than $2.15 a day. China shifted away from the command economy in 1979, and immediately began to experience the benefits. Most of the decline in poverty which preceded the explosive growth in the new millennium is attributed to land and agriculture reforms in the countryside.[11] China was followed by India in the 1980s. Her economy was opened to the dynamics of the market, but the socialist mentality was retained (complete with Five-Year Plans). The rising number of people in India living on less than $2.15-a-day was due to the good news—the number living in abject poverty (less than $1-a-day) decreased sharply in the 1990s.

It was a different story in Eastern Europe, however, where the USSR capitulated in 1991. This region fell into the open arms of the doctrine emanating from Washington and the International Mon-

Numbers of People Living Below $2.15 per day (millions)								
	1980	1984	1987	1990	1993	1996	1999	2001
China	875	813	730	824	802	649	627	593
E. Europe & Central Asia	20	18	14	23	81	97	112	93
India	630	661	697	731	769	805	804	826

Source: Chen and Ravallion (2004) table 3, p. 29

etary Fund (IMF). In the 1990s, during perestroika, the poverty trend had been downwards. Then, capitalism supplanted Marxism, and the number in poverty tragically escalated from 23m to 93m.

Whatever happened in China and India to improve the condition of the masses, to even a modest extent, the credit cannot be attributed to those in the West who promote schemes for eradicating poverty. The West's influence in those countries has been relatively weak. They exercise the deepest sway in Africa. And in sub-Sahara Africa, poverty rates also rose.

Human intelligence and material resources are available in abundance to afford decent living standards for everyone who wants to work, so no-one need suffer involuntary deprivation. Yet children die by the thousand every day for want of food. We want to know why. One thing is certain, however. We ought not to continue to rely for direction on economists (with certain exceptions) and the agencies that specialise in economic development, because theirs has been a 60-year record of unrealised aspirations. We maintain that they withheld the knowledge, from the people who need it, that would facilitate the economics of abundance.

Following World War II, economists began to model the way neo-colonial countries could develop. They were sincere in their endeavours, but their projects failed to lay the foundations for sustained growth. One of the doyens of this school, W Arthur Lewis, even claimed that "development must be inegalitarian".[12] Indeed, "higher levels of inequality were themselves seen as having beneficial implications for growth prospects".[13]

From then on, fashionable schools of thought came and went—four of them in all.[14] The UN valiantly intervened, but its initiatives were repeated disappointments. In 1977, the UN goal of universal access to water and sanitation had as its target date 1990—postponed to 2015; the universal primary school enrolment target date was also postponed to 2015. In 2005, the G7 countries promised to double foreign aid to Africa—the outcome was condemned as a farce by Bob Geldof in 2007. And the many IMF/World Bank initiatives, specific to countries that sought help, resulted in Structural Adjustment Programmes the outcome of which are controversial, to say the least.

The most recent school of thought highlights the way growth is affected by the distribution of land. After much dead-end theorising and hand-wringing, development economics has finally overturned one of its basic premises. Inequality is not inevitable, and attention should be paid to the links between growth and to equity in both its senses—as an asset (land), and norms of fairness.[15] But the pillars of conventional wisdom continue to resist the role of land in development. The World Bank, for example, has decided that it erred in focusing its financial resources on urban growth; and ought to retreat back to the countryside to try and help people living in poverty.[16] But under its new president, Robert Zoellick, it remains silent about the need for land reform, and remains wedded to conventional practices on taxation—the kind that actively obstruct the efficient use of land and labour in the countryside. The World Bank's doctrinal apparatus is a barrier to the clarity of thinking that is needed if poverty is to be abolished. For example, in acknowledging that small farms are more productive than large enterprises, it clouds the issues in mystery, by declaring that "markets are somehow not allocating the right amount of land to those who currently farm the smaller plots".[17] Note that word somehow. We shall demystify this alleged 'market' defect. We will explain that the biggest challenge is associated with the failures of governance.

Part 1
The Crisis of Philosophy

I

"The Most Important Economist in the World"

Jeffrey Sachs

He is the hero of people who campaign against world poverty. Jeffrey Sachs promises The End of Poverty. His best-selling treatise proclaims How We Can Make It Happen in Our Lifetime.

Presidents and prime ministers fete the economist who rubs shoulders with pop stars in the quest to eradicate the $1-a-day tragedy that blights the lives of a billion people. And that's not counting the further billion on $2-a-day, surviving at the margins of biological existence.

Professor Sachs is the man with the solutions in his portmanteau. That is why the New York Times dubbed him "probably the most important economist in the world",[1] an accolade that followed him on his flying missions around the world. And who can doubt the credentials of the man elevated to Special Advisor to the UN Secretary-General?

From Bolivia to Poland, from the mud huts of Malawi to the mega-cities of Asia—nowhere is beyond the reach of Jeffrey Sachs. What he doesn't know about helping people to grow out of poverty can't be worth knowing—can it? Sachs advises leaders in the neo-colonised world, guiding nations, with gusto, on how to escape the poverty traps that have defied all-powerful governments for generations.

Can it happen in our lifetime? If the secrets of balanced economic growth—in which income is allowed to trickle down to the poor—really are revealed in his lectures, delivered to star-struck audiences from Moscow to Delhi and Beijing, there would be no need for further exploration of the pervasiveness of poverty: we could leave it to Professor Sachs and the United Nations. Unfortunately, as we shall discover as we retrace his steps around the globe, Sachs is part of the problem. Today, the world is no closer to understanding the dynamics of poverty, let alone consigning it to history. Furthermore, we will explain how, insofar as the Sachs plan may succeed, the 21st century will witness the escalation of that brand of deep poverty that is the direct result of 'progress' in market economies.[2]

Jeffrey Sachs is not distracted by self-doubt, however. He exudes the confidence of a scholar who has command of his theory. But he also believes in taking the theory out into the real world. He acquired a taste for roaming around other people's countries, starting with Bolivia in 1985, and then jetting into Poland in 1989. We begin our story with his arrival in Russia in the summer of 1990, to give detailed briefings to Soviet planners on "the logic and key principles of market reforms".[3]

During the 1980s, Mikhail Gorbachev wanted to nudge the Soviet Union away from the clutches of centralised planning, but he failed to develop a credible strategy. Enter Jeffrey Sachs, who became advisor to the young English-speaking economists who were searching for a formula to transform the USSR from the command economy into—what?

Grigory Yavlinsky, as advisor to Gorbachev, needed guidance because, locked behind the Iron Curtain, Soviet economists had been schooled in a version of capitalism that was coloured by Marxist doctrines. Turning from state-directed production to consumer-sanctioned markets would be hazardous. The reformers needed policies informed by two considerations:

- An acute sensitivity to the culture and psychology of the peoples of Eastern Europe was imperative. Alien laws and institutions had to blend with their history and collective sentiments in a synthesis that would enable them to navigate to the good life beyond the Iron Curtain.
- A profound awareness of the shortcomings of market economics was a prerequisite. The last thing these vulnerable peoples needed was the incubation on their social soil of the kind of pathologies that cultivated poverty in the West.

Russian economists could not be expected to formulate, on their own, the laws and institutions of private enterprise. They wanted to emerge out of the near catatonic state to which civil society had been reduced by communism. Collaboration with Westerners was needed to merge the technical understanding of the inner workings of the market economy with the imagination that was needed to adapt state socialism. The privilege of undertaking this task fell to Jeffrey Sachs and several close colleagues. Armed with an introduction from philanthropist George Soros, Sachs met and worked with Yavlinsky before moving on to Yegor Gaidar, an advisor to Boris Yeltsin. Gaidar was to become Prime Minister of an independent Russia. Sachs contributed to the reform plan that shaped the first fatal days of this post-Soviet country.

Today, impoverished by the economics of the 'free market', many Russians regard themselves as victims of the plan that Jeffrey Sachs endorsed. His approach emphasised money and prices. His specialty at Harvard, where he was a professor of economics, was international finance and the macro-economics of the rich West. He now recalls:

> The initial shocks of price decontrol, currency convertibility, and market liberalisation could help, as such measures did in Poland, but they would not solve the problems of underlying structural disarray, falling energy supplies, and a myriad of other inter-connected crises. The reform measures, at their very best, would help to steer Russia on to a path of massive, generation-long economic and social transformation....Could it work? I thought so. I certainly thought it was worth a try.[4]

Sachs' work around the world was, by his own admission, the most challenging exercise in social engineering that could confront any economist, and yet it was approached without a first-hand understanding of "the contours of economic development and under-development in Latin America, Eastern Europe, and the former Soviet Union".[5] It was not until the early 1990s that he felt he had acquired such knowledge. And yet, he had already begun to brandish the key concepts—like liberalisation and privatisation—that the young advisors who were eager to acquire wisdom from the West would chant as magic mantras.

> My essential advice to Russia was to move quickly on the key reforms that were possible—such as stabilisation and market liberalisation—and to move definitively, although not overnight, on privatisation.[6]

Russia launched the reforms in January 1992. The plan became known as 'shock therapy'. Many people were to pay the price in the most fatal terms possible, as the graph shows.

Shock Therapy: Russia's Demographic Response

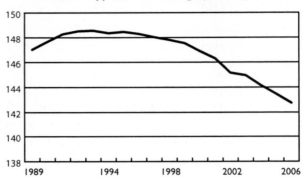

Life expectancy was reduced to the levels of the neo-colonised world. For men the average life expectancy in 1987 was 64.9 years. In 1994 this crashed to 57.5 years and in 2005 life expectancy remained below 60 years. The average life of women was also shortened, from more than 70 years (1987) to 65.3 years in 2005—the loss of an average of five years of life. Mortality rates eclipsed the fertility of the population, which succumbed to a demographic collapse unparalleled in any European country since the days of plague. The population reached its peak of 148.6m at the end of 1993, when Sachs ended his advisory role with the Russian government. From 1994, the shock effects of the 'therapy' administered under the tutelage of Western policy doctors saw the decimation of the population as it crashed by over 5m to 142.7m in 2006.

Sachs helped to lay the foundations for an approach to economic and social change that he carried back to New York. And there, in the corridors of the United Nations, he was given access to politicians and international civil servants who wanted to know how to eradicate poverty in the rest of the world.

UN Millennium Development Goals: Hope or Hoax?

While working in Moscow, Sachs proposed a transformation strategy that was composed of three main elements:

- A fund to stabilise the rouble.
- Cancellation of debts.
- Foreign aid, especially to help the most vulnerable individuals.

Sachs now points an accusing finger at financial institutions like the International Monetary Fund, and the richest nations (G7), for failing to fund his agenda. We need not doubt that his complaint has substance, that Western governments were more interested in transforming Russia into a compliant partner rather than renewing the strength of an enemy superpower.

Even so, Russia was rich in intellectual and natural resources. These could have been mobilised to facilitate her transformation, as China had done without the help of Western aid. So why did Russia fail? It failed because the Sachs model of economic development and the strategy for poverty alleviation were fatally flawed. Russia's endowment of talent was not harnessed to transform the nation. The Sachs emphasis on high finance as the cutting edge of change could not nourish the consensus that was needed to support the new institutions and bewildering practices that Russians were offered by President Yeltsin.

The crude monetarist model that was emphasised in Moscow in 1991 and 1992 could not lead the way to balanced transformation of the command economy, even if the international financiers had been generous with aid.[7] This proposition will be tested further as we explore the awesome challenges confronting poverty-stricken regions of Africa, Asia and South America. We will carry with us some of the memories of the turning points in Russia. Sachs spotlighted one of them: the Russian people fell foul of the failure of their state to protect them and the natural assets that could guarantee a flow of income into the public purse in perpetuity. The resource rents—the value of the gifts of nature—were available from the international markets to fund the restructuring of their economy and civil society. But during the two years 1995 and 1996, Sachs noted,

> Russian privatisation became a shameless and criminal activity. Essentially, a corrupt group of so-called businessmen, who later became known collectively as Russia's new oligarchs, were able to get their hands on tens of billions of dollars of natural resource wealth, mainly the oil and gas holdings of the Russian state. The best estimates are that about $100 billion of oil, gas, and other valuable commodities were transferred to private hands in return for perhaps no more than $1 billion of privatization receipts taken in by the Treasury.

The important point for us, in considering strategies for addressing poverty, is that there was nothing in the advice offered by Sachs which, in principle, could have prevented the sacking of Russia's riches. Provision needed to be made, philosophically, psychologically and constitutionally, to preserve the natural resources as the fund from which the people could draw to finance the new course on which they had embarked. No such provision was made in Sachs' plan for integrating Russia into the market economy. So even if the rouble had been stabilised, debts cancelled and aid had flowed in to help pensioners, the absence of the appropriate fiscal policy meant that the state would have been vulnerable to the plunder that did, indeed, ensue.[9]

With hindsight, would Sachs have offered a different plan of campaign for Russia? We are, after all, entitled to learn from experience. Ten years later—now celebrated as "probably the most important economist in the world"—would he have modified his advice? Learning from the past was vital, for during the intervening decade his brief was extended to encompass most of the rest of the world. He roamed through the academic auditoriums and the political corridors of power in India and China and—the greatest accolade imaginable—he was mandated by the United Nations. With the prestige and power of the UN behind him, surely he would be able to succeed where sovereign governments had failed? Much depended, of course, on how the nature of poverty was characterised, if more than a televised band aid was to be applied.

To achieve the UN Millennium Development Goal of redeeming humanity by abolishing the $1-a-day syndrome, Sachs set to work by combining the scientific resources of Columbia University's Earth Institute, which he directed, with the practical knowledge of UN teams scattered around the world. Would Sachs' advice help governments to achieve sustainable growth? Would he have prescribed alternative policies if he had relived his three years in Moscow? We are left in no doubt: "To a large extent, the answer is no."[10]

As the Director of the UN's Millennium Project, Sachs exercised extraordinary influence. But debt cancellation and foreign aid could not be any more successful than what happened in Russia, where the people were excluded from their equal share of the oil and gas rents that the oligarchs now use to buy football clubs and real estate in the West. At the heart of the problem of poverty is a reality that was not acknowledged by Sachs, his co-workers or the international agencies that deploy massive financial power and material resources in their attacks on poverty. Under the policies that determine the distribution of income in the capitalist economy, poverty is an institutionalised by-product of economic growth. We shall see that growth-oriented investment retards people's development, if it is not combined with changes to the tax laws that determine the primary distribution of income.

India: Progress with Poverty

In assessing the conditions that create poverty today, it is imperative that we do not forget the influence of the past.Disentangling the present from the influences inherited from those who lived long ago is daunting; but it has been achieved for India in a remarkable piece of research by two students of that country's colonial legacy. Their method for excavating the impact of the past on the present exposes how the practices and institutions of sovereign nations are continuing the exploitation that was supposed to be terminated by independence.

The British East India Company arrived in 1613 to launch the exploitation of the sub-continent for resources to fund first the opulent lifestyles of the aristocracy and then the industrialisation of the British economy.

With independence in 1947, India's leaders opted for socialism and centrally directed Five-Year Plans. The figure below reveals the outcome: the prosperity that the people of a post-colonial nation expected did not materialise. Under socialism, growth did not eradicate poverty, which remained the norm.

Historic Growth of the Indian Economy

Sources: Maddison (1995) and Sachs (2005) p. 181

Then, in 1970, came the Green Revolution. The West promoted a poverty-eliminating strategy based on increasing the food yields of peasants in the countryside. This did raise the profits of foreign corporations that held the patents on genetically engineered seeds and the pesticides which, for the peasants, were an expensive addition to the cost of producing food. Finally, in 1991, India turned from socialism to capitalism. Market reforms were adopted and India joined the other former socialist countries to expand and integrate the global market.

Independence did not deliver universal prosperity because India continued to live under the legacy of her former colonial masters. But how do we measure the impact of that past? Those two students of India's colonial legacy, Abhijit Banerjee and Lakshmi Iyer—economists at the Massachusetts Institute of Technology—employed advanced statistical tools. They identified the role of the British in exacerbating an already skewed distribution of wealth by creating the legal framework that continues to prejudice people's life chances today.

Given the post-independence poverty levels, they asked, how could the marked differences in income distribution, welfare and public investment within India be explained? They divided the sub-continent's regions into three categories, according to the method instituted by the British to extract rents between the 18th and 20th centuries. The table over shows the regions.

Land Tax-paying Regions, India (1757-1947)		
Zamindari (landlords)	Raiyatwari (cultivators)	Mahalwari (villages)
Bengal Bihar Orissa Tamil Nadu Andhra Pradesh	Madras Bombay Assam	North-West Provinces Panjab

The 'landlord' regions came into existence because the British misread tribal customs and turned chiefs into landowners for their revenue-collecting convenience. But in the regions where the British collected rents direct from the cultivators, they consolidated the tenure rights of the peasants. For some regions, however, they respected common ownership rights by levying rents on villages as a whole, leaving the villagers to determine how much each of them would pay.

Significantly, the soils of the landlord regions were more fertile compared with areas farmed under the other two rent-revenue models. This ought to have meant that the cultivators in these regions would prosper relative to the others. That is not what happened. For the British re-invested more of the rents in the infrastructure of the areas from which they collected revenue directly from the cultivators. The outcome, a century or more later, was clearly traceable in the levels of investment and in yields. The differences were to exercise profound consequences in the late 20th century. Some of these are summarised in the table opposite.

Inequality in 1885 was lower in those districts where the British collected rents direct from cultivators than in the landlord districts. And canal construction was funded by the British almost exclusively in the non-landlord areas. Looking at modern-day India, Banerjee and Iyer note: "The effects we document are surprisingly large, given that we are looking at an institution that no longer exists".

The British Legacy in Post-Colonial India	
Categories	Cultivator & Village indices compared with Landlord regions
Irrigation	25% higher
Fertiliser use	45% higher
High-yielding rice varieties	25% higher
Agricultural productivity	16% higher, overall with crop yields: Rice: 17% higher Wheat: 23% higher*
Village schools availability	20-60% higher
Literacy rates	18% higher
Infant mortality	40% lower

Source: Banerjee and Iyer (2005)

* Estimates for differences in yields took into account geographic variables and the duration of British rule.

The lessons are many and varied, but we need to focus on the issues that help us to understand the causes of poverty today.

First, the British were not in India on a benevolent mission. Why, then (for example) would they invest in local irrigation networks?

The answer: self-interest. In 1841, the land tax yielded 60% of total British government revenue extracted out of the sub-continent. So investing in the infrastructure increased the rental yields. The returns were not as buoyant from the landlord districts, however, because the rent collectors (the landlords) pocketed as much of the rents as they could for themselves. So fertile high-yielding regions generated lower revenues, per acre, for the British, than the marginal soils from which rents were tapped direct from cultivators and the village commons. Consequently, the British concentrated on improving the irrigation networks of the poor soils from which they could extract a higher proportion of the rents for Britain.

The landlords, on the other hand, grew richer as they privatised a growing proportion of the rents during the 19th century. And they had no legal obligation or economic incentive to reinvest in the welfare of their tenants.

> This meant that the colonial state had more at stake in the economic prosperity of non-landlord areas, since this could be translated into higher rents. This is reflected in an increasing number of legislations trying to protect the peasants from money-lenders…It also meant that the state had more reason to invest in these areas in irrigation, railways, schools and other infrastructure…[A]lmost all canals constructed by the British were in non-landlord areas. If indeed these areas had better public goods when the British left, it is plausible that they could continue to have some advantage even now.[11]

Historians have been puzzled by the large and often growing differences across the states of India, but Banerjee and Iyer have elegantly identified the core explanation. The landlord areas were drained of a larger proportion of the rents, the reciprocal of which was higher rates of illiteracy and child mortality. By not using landlords as rent-collecting intermediaries in the other regions, however, the British had greater incentive to reinvest rents in ways that would benefit the lives of those who paid the land tax direct to government. One outcome, today, after all this time, is that non-landlord areas, in spite of their natural disadvantage, continue to out-perform the landlord regions in productivity terms. Poverty reduction in modern India is higher in non-landlord areas. Scholars will continue to argue about causal mechanisms, but Banerjee and Iyer are sure of one fact.

> What seems clear is that the concentration of economic and political power in the hands of an elite, resulting from the landlord-based land tenure system, continues to be a heavy burden on the economic life of these areas.[12]

Enter Jeffrey Sachs. He arrived in 1994—having just resigned as the Russian government's advisor—to promote his doctrine of liberalisation. His audiences were sceptical. But by the end of the century India did deliver remarkable growth rates. Did this validate the doctrine of capitalism? Sachs thought so, and he was pleased to see his proposals adopted in Delhi.

> We were delighted when the Prime Minister proclaimed [our] objectives in his message to the nation on August 15, 2000. The goal of at least 8% per year economic growth…was subsequently endorsed by India's Planning Commission.[13]

But millions of people failed to share in the good times. Why? And why did the voters eject the government in the election of 2004, "reflecting a massive vote for change emerging from India's countryside"?[14]

India was in the clutches of the growth disease—of progress associated with the poverty that was caused by 'progress'. This process began during the Green Revolution, which Sachs calls 'rural-led development'. Incomes were raised for a segment of the population, but this triggered a response that is part of the DNA of the modern capitalist economy. Peasants were required to pay higher rents to their landlords. If money was to be made out of the increased productivity delivered by bio-science, that money was not going to trickle down to those who toiled in the fields. Increases in the costs of fertiliser and seeds, and rents, locked the peasants in the classic trap. For many of them this had one fatal outcome: indebtedness, from which they could not escape. So began the suicides and the displacement of yet more people from the land. They had no choice but to migrate to the nearest city.[15]

The tragedy that unfolded in the countryside is told by the numbers of people seeking refuge in urban slums. The pressure was intense in Mumbai, where 60% of the population now live in slums. In the two decades of India's economic growth, the number of slum dwellers doubled, rising from 27.9m in 1981 to 61.8m in 2001 according to Kumari Selja, the Minister for Housing and Urban Poverty Alleviation.

The process of redistributing income from those who produce it to people who (as land owners) do not add value to the wealth of the nation, as illustrated by India, is inscribed into the fabric of the capitalist economy.[16] This is not a law of nature. It is sanctioned by one of two circumstances.

• Privatisation of rental income. This is what enriched the aristocracy in late feudal Britain, and the zamindaris of colonial India.
• Redistribution by default. If the right of producers to an equal

share of the rents they produce is not protected by law, the state's failure is exploited by opportunists. This is what enriched the oligarchs in Yeltsin's Russia.

India, as a victim of the colonial rent grab, first sought solace in socialism after independence. History has pronounced its verdict on this model. But why is the market economy also failing hundreds of millions of Indians? In 1976, the government formulated the Urban Land (Ceiling & Regulation) Act. This sought to socialise vacant land in towns to prevent the concentration of sites in the hands of profiteering speculators. Legislators realised that distortions in the market for real estate had damaging social effects. One of these was identified by Nipun Vaid in his assessment of the Act.

> Distortions in the land market often lead to land speculation which is a scenario in which the value of land is artificially raised beyond actual price and after this bubble of inflation bursts, investors in land lose out on capital as prices in the market fall.[17]

Imposing ceilings on the ownership of land, however, with the owners regulated by law and administered by civil servants, failed to deliver the benefits of an efficient property market. The Act was ordered to be deleted from the law books in 2004. The Minister of Housing and Urban Poverty Alleviation admitted that "the complexities of urban administration have grown manifold due to urban growth, population concentration, mounting poverty and unplanned spatial activities".[18]

Given such policy failures, how do we explain the extraordinary growth rates in the decade up to 2008? They were (ironically) predicated on another colonial legacy: language. The extensive use of English, combined with information technology and low wages, made it possible to service directly the needs of Western corporations.

But even as software writers prospered, their cousins in the countryside—and notably those in the regions dominated by landlords—sank deeper into debt. Someone—or something— had to be blamed. Jeffrey Sachs resorted to the device that is employed by ideologues to shut down debate about competing doctrines. He claimed that an anti-poverty 'silver bullet' did not exist. In his own words, there were "no 'magic bullets', no single solution that will put an end to global poverty".[19]

If Sachs was correct, he needed a scapegoat for poverty. He found it in resource rents. Another economist who specialised in economic development, Oxford University's Professor Paul Collier, recalled:

> Economist Jeffrey Sachs revived concern about the problem of natural resource rents. Since then political scientists have joined in, suggesting that resource revenues worsen governance.[20]

The Curse of the Resource Rents was unleashed by "the most important economist in the world". Paul Collier set out to investigate whether it was true: is nature a "curse"? Is it to blame for the blight on the lives of the billion poorest people on earth?

2

Blame it on Nature

Doctrine of the Resource Curse

B laming others is a ploy that has been with us from the beginning of psychological time.

The Reverend Thomas Malthus diverted respon-sibility
away from the architects of poverty in 19th century Britain, blaming the victims for their plight. To his way of thinking people on
low incomes are responsible for failing to control their sexual ap-
petites. They reproduce beyond their ability to clothe and feed
their children.

For many people, hardship in a world with a billion people sub-
sisting on less than $1-a-day needs to be explained in terms that are
reassuring. But if we do not wish to blame the poor, a metaphysical
explanation needs to be conjured up. Nature has now been elected
as the proximate culprit. Starving children, their shocking images
portrayed on TV news programmes, are the victims of a "curse".

The thesis that nature is to blame has been endorsed by Jeffrey
Sachs. His thesis was taken up by billionaire philanthropist George
Soros and others, and received scholarly analysis by Paul Collier

at Oxford, where he directs the Centre for the Study of African Economies.

Sachs and his collaborators showed that countries rich in natural resources tended to grow more slowly than those that were resource poor. This was the curse that nature apparently inflicted on populations that were unlucky enough to occupy territories endowed with oil, diamonds and gold.[1] Sachs explored the "roots of failure in natural resource-led development", and the curse turned out to be the villain.

Sophisticated statistical analysis led him to the conclusion that "empirical support for the curse of natural resources is not bullet proof, but it is quite strong".[2] We shall show that blaming nature's munificence is a travesty.

- Land-rich Costa Rica did not suffer from a resource curse in the 18th century.[3]
- Gold-rich Australia did not suffer from a resource curse in the 19th century (see pages 143-149).
- Diamond-rich Botswana did not suffer from a resource curse in the 20th century (see pages 49-58).

These, and other cases, demonstrate that to talk in terms of a "curse" merely distracts politicians who are looking for an excuse to avoid their obligations. Sachs missed something. In the cases that we cite, the populations that harnessed their natural resources for the common good adopted tenure-and-tax policies that facilitated economic growth. The economic rents were not allowed to distort society and retard growth; in fact, they were harnessed to fund growth.

Paul Collier investigated the so-called resource curse after moving to Oxford from the World Bank, where he served as Director of

Development Research. The sincerity with which he addresses the plight of the billion people on the lowest incomes is not doubted. And he does not pull his punches in his account of what needs to be done to help them out of the poverty trap. But an escape plan that fails to identify the starting point is liable to lead down a cul-de-sac.

Poverty is at its deepest in the 50 states around the world where, despite strenuous efforts by international aid agencies, the route out of poverty is strewn with seemingly insurmountable traps. Who is to blame for the corruption and civil conflicts that blight people's lives? What Collier describes as "paradoxical" is "the discovery of valuable natural resources in the context of poverty".[4]

> The heart of the resource curse is that resource rents make democracy malfunction.

According to Collier, rents—such as those from oil—"have substantially reduced the likelihood that a society is democratic". So damaging were the riches of nature that the professor concluded that "without natural resource surpluses, democracies outgrow autocracies" (emphasis added). To drive home the implicit thesis that poverty-stricken populations in Africa would be better off without the flow of rents, he declared that

> In the absence of natural resource surpluses a fully democratic polity outperforms a despotic autocracy by around 2% per year. By the time natural resource rents are around 8% of national income, the growth advantage of democracy has been eliminated. Beyond this the net effect of democracy is adverse. Taking a country with resource rents worth 20% of national income, the switch from autocracy to intense electoral competition would lower the growth rate by nearly 3%.

There is apparently much to curse about nature's generosity in providing resource rents! Here is an explanation for poverty and civil strife that relieves the human race of guilt. The doctrine of the resource curse is treated as a serious scholastic theory, and Professor Collier devoted serious research time to exploring the problem. With co-worker Anke Hoeffler, he estimated the rents generated by natural resources, country by country and year by year. He correctly defined rents as the excess of revenues after deducting the costs of production. This was a careful exercise, because the size of the economic surplus varies for a long list of reasons. He explains:

> Estimating the rents on primary commodities is an important advance on just counting their value: the rent on $1m of oil exports is much greater than the rent on $1m of coffee exports because the costs of production are much lower. So data on primary commodity exports, which is what people had used when they had bothered to look at the numbers, are a poor guide to how valuable the resources really are. And even $1m of oil exports generates a bigger surplus if it is coming from an easy-to-exploit onshore location than if it is deep offshore, and if the price per barrel is $60 rather than $10.[5]

Collier and Hoeffler compared the flow of rents with political institutions and drew the conclusion that rents "both undermine governance, and are dysfunctional in the context of poor governance". Thus, by this logic, resource rents undermine the checks and balances in democracy (such as press freedom) "and thereby facilitate patronage politics, reducing public goods provision in the process". When the rent tap is turned on, altruism is subordinated to embezzlement for private gain. Ill-informed voters are manipulated by their leaders in the quest for the power that gives privileged access to the easy life funded by rents.

Collier and Hoeffler decided that it was easier for the public to control their leaders when they had to pay taxes, because this encouraged people to scrutinise what was done in their name. But resource rents, apparently, do not inspire citizen scrutiny. It gets worse for those countries that are well-endowed by nature. For as rents increase, government can lower the revenue received from taxes on people's wages and savings. This consequently reduces the level of public scrutiny of politicians, "and so the rate of embezzlement is higher".

This is, indeed, a bleak scenario. One would think that the riches of nature would help to banish poverty. Not so, it seems, based on the way scholars like Collier analyse the role of rent. It appears that governments welcome the opportunity to raise revenue from resource rents instead of by taxing people because this enables them to escape public scrutiny. As a result, those governments are under less pressure to provide public services. Depressingly, Collier and Hoeffler conclude that "comparing two societies with the same level of income but with different shares of natural resource rents, the one with the higher share will have the worse provision of public goods".

From this, it would appear that the rich West has been doing the poor nations a favour by relieving them of their resource rents and of urging them to raise tax revenue from labour and capital instead. After all, as Collier and Hoeffler note, "democracy enhances growth except in the presence of substantial natural resources where they retard it". To stress the point, they explain that "in the absence of resource rents democracy is good for growth".

And as it happens, that is what the policies prescribed by agencies like the World Bank and the IMF have achieved. The doctrine that relieved the neo-colonial countries of resource rents is known as The Washington Consensus.

Colonialism by Other Means

when formal colonialism came to an end, European powers retreated without unscrambling the institutions that they had bequeathed. The jurisdiction of the imperial powers was withdrawn, but the expectation continued that they would enjoy privileged access to the resources that attracted them to the distant lands in the first place. Preferential treatment was secured to exploit the benefits that flowed from the preservation of the granite pillars of the West's social architecture, the property laws and the related financial institutions which remained embedded in the soils of the former colonies.

Could this be the reason why so many countries remained locked in poverty? A mathematically rigorous approach to examining this question was employed by Daron Acemoglu and his associates at the Massachusetts Institute of Technology and the University of California (Berkeley).

Acemoglu, a professor of economics, went in search of what he, too, called root causes. Using algebra and the best data available, he concluded that the colonial project was one designed to enrich the European colonists. The settlers chose those institutions that best served their interests. Where they were not able or willing to settle in other people's territories, "they introduced or maintained existing extractive institutions when it was in their interest to extract resources from the non-European populations of the colonies, as in much of Africa, central America, the Caribbean, and South Asia".[6] The common theme that runs through the prolific work of Acemoglu and his colleagues is the role of rent in the fate of nations, both during and after colonialism.

In almost all cases, we can link the persistence of extractive institutions

> to the fact that, even after independence, the elites in these societies had a lot to lose from institutional reform. Their political power and claim to economic rents rested on the existing extractive institutions...[7]

Territories that were rich before the arrival of Europeans suffered a reversal of fortune, and ended up being impov-erished. They were the victims of the extractive process by which the colonists leeched the economic rents out of the country. In contrast, a different strategy was employed in those territories that were sparsely populated and where disease was not a threat to Europeans. Here, the settlers replicated the institutions that favoured economic growth. Acemoglu discovered that variables such as geography (for example, locations in the tropics) did not account for the different institutional strategies that were employed by Europeans.

Others—such as Jeffrey Sachs—claimed that poverty could be explained, in part, by the proximity of a country to the equator. Acemoglu et al demonstrate that, once they factored institutions into the equation, "countries in Africa or those closer to the equator do not have lower incomes".[8] Similarly, the Sachs thesis that diseases such as malaria affect economic development was also incorrect. People who lived in high malaria-prone areas developed immunity, so the disease would have little direct effect on the economic performance of the indigenous populations.[9]

Advocates of foreign aid (like Sachs) were missing something crucial. Acemoglu et al, in searching for the fundamental causes of the large differences in income per capita between countries, spotlighted the role of institutions. In particular, they subjected property rights to forensic interrogation. Popular hypotheses on the causes of poverty were rejected in favour of the role of private property. This, apparently, was the key factor that encouraged investment and economic growth while diminishing corruption and civil conflict. Their analysis is convincing, but they admitted that many questions were left unanswered. In particular, their "institutions are treated largely as a 'black box'".[10] That mysterious box, which serves to conceal the true nature of the institutions they are dealing with, needs to be levered open.

We believe that Acemoglu et al. failed to identify the root causes of poverty because their model of institutions is too simplistic. They employ a concept of property rights that fails to reflect the rich texture of the institutions that were adopted by European settlers in foreign lands. As we shall see in chapter 6, significant differences in strategies were employed.

A more complex analytical framework is needed, which we have stylised in the figure opposite. On the horizontal axis we locate the institutions that favour (at one extreme) the predatory tactics of the colonists dedicated to extracting resource rents— such as absentee gold mine owners—in contrast to, for example, Europeans who settled and invested in the local economy. On the vertical scale we locate property rights. Anthropologically speaking, people have traditionally recognised that property falls into two categories: those rights that are personal, and those rights that inhere in the community. How else could a community function, if it did not have a claim on output? The traditional allocation was based on the difference between property rights that delivered incomes that were earned, as opposed to those that were designated as unearned. The policies that flow naturally from this distinction are elaborated in Part 3. At one extreme of our figure's scale are the simple private rights to which Acemoglu draws attention. At the other end of the scale are the complex rights which disaggregate the benefits that flow from property.

A sophisticated theory of property rights and economic activity offers a deeper explanation of the root causes of that poverty which

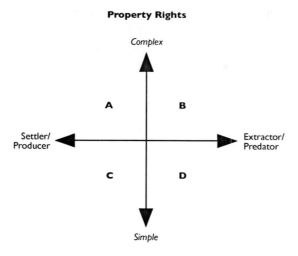

Property Rights

Complex

A   B

Settler/ ◄──────────────────► Extractor/
Producer   Predator

C   D

Simple

is pre-determined by institutional arrangements. With our frame-work, we can fill in the pieces that are hidden in Acemoglu's 'black box'. Thus, we would place 19th century Australia (see p. 143) in the A quadrant of the figure, while 19th century Argentina's institutions (see p. 140) would locate it in the C quadrant. We understand that the manner in which the resource rents were distributed shaped the fate of indigenous populations and the new settlers. So we can account for the persistence of poverty today.

Unfortunately, however, absence of agreement among social scientists about the fundamental issues means that, after 250 years of scientific economic reasoning, there is little consensus on what delivers prosperity. Sachs, for example, admits that economists could not agree about what drove economic growth, and "we have a similar diversity of views on the natural resource question. In other words, a complete answer to what is behind the curse of natural resources therefore awaits a better answer to the question about what ultimately drives growth".[11]

In our view, the decomposition of economics into

fragmented schools of thought is the logical consequence of the refusal to integrate into theory the spatial context of life, represented, in economics, by the concepts of land and rent. This spatial dimension, however, is obscured because economists insist on treating them as 'capital' and 'profits'. Consequently, given present-day thinking, it is unlikely that even mighty global agencies such as the UN will formulate a coherent strategy capable (in principle) of delivering prosperity and peace on a sustained basis.

Our hypothesis is that people have the power to create that prosperity for themselves. So our challenge is: what is stopping them?

People-Power Rents: A Sub-Saharan Paradigm

Africa's bleak history of neo-colonialism is legend, but the clues to prosperity can be excavated from that past with the aid of the right tools.

Botswana, for example, has performed remarkably well compared to her sub-Saharan neighbours. Why? The country's per capita income of nearly $10,000 far exceeds what others are achieving (see table below). There is even better news, however. Botswana is free of civil conflicts. She has enjoyed democracy for the last 40 years. Contrary to the Sachs resource curse thesis, and the Collier democracy thesis, this country effected a successful transition to post-colonial sovereignty.

Five Sub-Saharan African Countries: selected indices (2006)

	Botswana	Namibia	Uganda	Zambia	Malawi
Incomepercapita (US$)	9,945	7,418	1,478	943	646
Top income tax rate (%)	25	35	30	37.5	40
Topcorporatetax rate (%)	25	35	30	35	30
Tax revenue (% of GDP)	36.9	27.3	11.7	17.6	20.1
Population (millions)	1.8	2	27.8	11.5	12.6
Unemployment (%)	23.8	34	n/a	50	n/a

Source: Kane, Holmes and O'Grady (2007)

Botswana is rich in diamonds, gold, nickel and copper, yet she does not suffer from the resource curse. She is also land-locked, which according to Sachs is supposed to be a constraint on economic growth. This is a country with relatively low tax rates and high public spending on school and health services; and it is ranked as Africa's least corrupt country, with one of the world's highest average growth rates over the past four decades. Here is a puzzle that needs explaining. Can we open Acemoglu's 'black box' to discover why Botswana is a model for her neighbours?

The IMF posed the question: Did Botswana escape from the resource curse? "Resource rents tend to bring about not only conflict but also corruption."[12] Botswana, however, dedicated her resource rents to investment in public infrastructure under a fiscal discipline called the Sustainable Budget Index. In addition, government channels rents into the Pula Fund, which invests for the long-term benefit of the nation. But why does Botswana's government behave in this public-spirited way instead of dissipating rents in corruption and conflict? This was the question addressed by Daron Acemoglu and his colleagues. They conclude that Botswana had good institutions, which they define as institutions of private property.[13] They stress the importance of the individual.

> How did these various features of Botswana's history and political situation affect the design of its institutions? To answer this question, we first have to note that institutions are ultimately the endogenous creation of individuals. Institution building, therefore, has to be analysed within the context of the interests of the actors and the constraints facing them.[14]

We shall explain in chapter 3 that this stress on the role of the individual is a serious misrepresentation of reality. It understates the role of institutions and culture in general, in enabling people to make decisions that are of mutual benefit to everyone in the community. The primary example is the provision of what economists call 'public goods'—the shared services (public health, transportation) that we need as we go about our daily lives.

The key, in this case, was noted by Acemoglu and his colleagues: the colonising British did not unravel traditional tribal practices. But nor did they invest in the territory's infrastructure. So when colonial rule ended in 1966, the country was much as it was before the intrusion of Europeans. The outcome was the survival of tribal institutions that encouraged broad participation in decision-making and traditional constraints on tribal leaders. But what, precisely, disciplined the people and their leaders to ensure good economic policies when, "in the rest of Africa, good economics is often bad politics—ie, good economic policies often do not generate enough rents for politicians, or they make it more likely that the government will be overthrown".[15] Acemoglu et al employ mathematics to compare the institutions of a variety of countries to conclude that effective property rights which are associated with institutions of private property (their emphasis), provide the answer: success in Botswana was not due to the rich resource endowment but good institutions.

Those institutions reach back to pre-colonial times, when "land was collectively owned [and] cattle were privately owned".[16] Following independence the government passed the Mines and Minerals Act (1967). This vested sub-soil mineral rights in the national government, at a time when the country had one abattoir, two secondary schools and few paved roads. Then diamonds were discovered, followed by copper and nickel. The spectacular record of social development was the consequence, because "these resource rents have been invested rather than squandered".[17]

> Diamond rents were widely distributed and the extent of this wealth increased the opportunity cost of undermining the good institutional path—no group wanted to fight to expand its rents at the expense of 'rocking the boat'.[18]

But to what do we attribute the cultural ethos which facilitated the diffusion of rents, through government, in a way that raised investment in infrastructure? Acemoglu et al insist that this was the result of "an underlying set of institutions—institutions of private property—that encouraged investment and economic development".[19] Our competing thesis is that it was the traditional ethic of sharing land—of collective property rights in the resources of nature (land), but not of capital (cattle)—that explains Botswana's remarkable achievement.

In 1980, a survey of property rights in land was presented by a politician who was to become Deputy Speaker of the Botswana legislature. BK Temane described three distinct land tenure systems. Freehold land represented 6% of the total. State land covered 23% of the territory, and 71% was designated as tribal land.

> Historically, all land in Botswana was vested in the Chiefs of various tribes to be held in trust for members of that tribe. Land was allocated by the Chiefs' representatives—the ward head and sub-ward heads upon application by tribesmen. Membership in a given tribe ensured an individual's right of access to tribal land for his use.[20]

After independence, tribal arrangements were preserved through the Tribal Land Act (1968). Modifications, such as the Tribal

Grazing Policy, were undertaken only after extensive consultations through the kgotla (village) meetings, so people were able to influence legislation. Land boards were created and land allocated on the basis of leases of 50 years (renewable). "The leaseholder is also subject to a rent on the land payable to the land board, subject to review every five years," reported Temane.[21]

In the tribal land tenure system, "speculation in land is avoided and even the poorest member of the tribe is not 'landless'".[22] Freehold tenure in towns was regarded as a "relic of the colonial past. It is now considered inappropriate to grant freehold title as this deprives the state of any future say in the ownership of the land unless it is acquired compulsorily".[23] Problems continued which needed to be addressed, particularly the attitude of financial institutions that favoured freehold property rights. Nonetheless, Botswana succeeded in achieving what was exceptional in sub-Sahara Africa simply because the British just did not covet a territory that was blighted by the Kalahari Desert. As a result, tribal property rights secure the individual's access to the community's land in the post-colonial era. Thus, land was not a contested asset.

There was, however, one risk: economic growth would result in the rise in the value of urban land. This could lead to the inequities that are the institutionalised cause of poverty in the West. Botswana addressed that issue.

Government, tribe or state 'ownership' of the land in the ultimate, ensures that land values are increased if at all for the community's benefit and that community investment does not unevenly favour some individuals simply because they happen to own some land.[24]

Thus, social stability and economic growth were achieved not because of institutions that stressed private property rights. Rather, the success may be attributed to a more complex, sophisticated philosophy of property: the conjunction of individual and community rights in a form that harmonises private and social interests. Thus, in terms of our figure of property rights (on p. 47 above), Botswana would be located towards the north-west corner of quadrant A.

Botswana did not suffer a resource curse—of private corruption and public conflict—because rents, in the main, were reserved for the community's benefit. This was achieved because society preserved a customary sense of the right of everyone to share the riches of nature. The economic surplus would be diffused through the public sector while, through the tax system, the weakest burden possible was imposed on capital investment in private enterprise.

Two caveats need introduced. First, countries that are not rich in natural resources are not automatically disadvantaged compared to a country like Botswana (see box opposite).

Second, it would be a mistake to idealise the Botswana model and thereby overlook residual problems. We will identify one, the case of the Kalahari Bushmen (see box over). This illustrates how even an enlightened government can intrude on people's land rights—ostensibly in the name of the public good. This means that, unless the individual can enforce rights against government without those rights being manipulated, there is a risk of losing one's natural right of access to use land.

But the most important lesson to be carried out of Botswana comes from an incident that occurred at the critical historical juncture when the country became independent. This was the time of greatest vulnerability for the indigenous population in terms

Rent & People-Power

ACCORDING to George Soros, drawing on the teachings of Jeffrey Sachs, "There is not much that one can do about bad location".* Wrong. Where nature is parsimonious, people-power can com-pensate. This is achieved by harnessing location to everyone's mutual benefit.

Most of Botswana's neighbours are not richly endowed by nature. Does this account for the poor performance of countries like Uganda and Zambia? The rent issue needs to be explored much more deeply, for resource-poor countries like Malawi and Uganda have riches of another kind: people.

People represent human energy and creativity. This people power can generate the surplus that is a rental value every bit as vital in raising living standards as the minerals buried beneath Botswana's territory. The major difference is that oil, diamonds and gold are finite resources. One day they will be exhausted. Rent created by the fusion of people-power is infinite. Particle for particle, rent generated by people as if from nothing is the most benign source of revenue. Those rents are most evident in towns, where people are willing to pay to occupy bare surfaces that have no attributes beyond their location.

With this knowledge, can we elaborate a model of growth that includes eve-ryone's interests? Conventional economists and Western governments are aware of the key elements of that model, which would release the power of the billions who live in poverty. These people *could* generate creative energy sufficient to eclipse anything delivered by nuclear fission. But Western policy advisers, as they cruise the world's regions of deprivation, remain silent. You may find occasional traces of this knowledge in the academic literature, but where is the systematic effort to inform the people? Instead, emphasis is placed on the doctrines of the post-classical model of economics. This purposefully degrades knowledge of rent.** The consequence is institutionalised poverty, the corruption of culture, and civil wars.

* Soros (2004) p. 111   ** Gaffney and Harrison (1994)

of the capacity to build a post-tribal politicised society that was capable of taking its place among the international community of nations.

Botswana then had a per capita GDP of $100. Would the people be free to enjoy the fruits of their natural resources in a sovereign state? Diamonds lay beneath the desert, and these could fund the services that would raise standards of health and welfare. But they lacked the technology to extract and market the diamonds, so they would need foreign assistance. In stepped de Beers, the South African diamond cartel. What happened then is told by Joseph Stiglitz in Globalisation and its Discontents.

> Shortly after independence, the cartel paid Botswana $20m for a diamond concession in 1969, which reportedly returned $60m in profits a year. In other words, the payback period was four months![25]

Unfortunately for de Beers, the government of Botswana then enlisted the help of a lawyer from the World Bank. He argued forcefully for a renegotiation of the contract. The mining interests were outraged. Under dispute was a huge flow of rental income.

> De Beers...tried to tell people that Botswana was being greedy. They used what political muscle they could, through the World Bank, to stop him [the lawyer]. In the end, they managed to extract a letter from the World Bank making it clear that the lawyer did not speak for the Bank. Botswana's response: That is precisely why we are listening to him.[26]

The dispute was resolved with the discovery of a second large diamond deposit. This enabled Botswana to renegotiate the whole commercial relationship with de Beers—to the mutual benefit of both parties.

Tribal Land Rights

THE Bushmen of the Kalahari Desert were immune from rent-seekers—until diamonds were discovered under one of their settlements. The government denied wanting to resettle the hunter-gatherers to clear the way for mining. The Bushmen were sceptical. A legal battle secured them victory in 2006: under the Constitution, they were entitled to remain on their ancestral lands.

Chapter 2 of the Botswana Constitution protects people from being deprived of their land. Tribal property is also secured to prevent the National Assembly from enacting any law that might affect tribal organisation. The Bushmen thought that they could continue to use their hunting grounds following their legal victory. But the government decided to amend the Constitution by deleting a passage from the Chapter (paragraph 3(c) of Section 14). This provision affords protection by regulating entry into or residence within areas occupied by Bushmen. By deleting this clause, the government hoped to relocate the Bushmen, ostensibly to provide them with the social care that was not available in the middle of the desert.

The London-based Survival International argue that this legal ploy would not render the Bushmen vulnerable to dispossession of their territory—for Section 14 (1) reads: "No person shall be deprived of his freedom of movement...freedom [meaning] the right to move freely throughout Botswana, the right to reside in any part of Botswana..."

The Bushmen case is one of a growing list of legal test cases that protect traditional land rights in countries like Canada, Australia, South Africa and Malaysia. But uncertainties about the status of the rights of people who wish to live according to tribal customs stresses the need to resolve the property rights of everyone, including the first settlers on territories who wish to preserve their customary ways of life.

In this episode we see how easy it would have been for Botswana to go down the route to mass poverty. It was the intervention of a "brilliant and dedicated lawyer", seconded to the government by the World Bank (which then denied him), which rescued the country from a predatory deal. Without that intervention, the extra millions of dollars would not have made much difference to the fabulous profits of the diamond cartel. But those rents made the difference between poverty and prosperity for hundreds of thousands of people in Botswana.

To lay the solid institutional foundations for growth and prosperity, the peoples of the neo-colonised world need to instruct their governments to undertake a renegotiation over their nation's rents similar to what happened in Botswana. For the redevelopment of their societies rests exclusively on coming to terms with a richer understanding of the meaning of rent as public value.

3

A Theory of Corruption

The Corruption of Rent as Public Value

To understand the making of poverty, both in the poor neo-colonised countries and in the rich West, we need a theory of corruption.

We have seen how social scientists now focus on the damage that is caused by the misuse of rent. As it happens, that economic concept is the most analytically fruitful tool for understanding the processes at work.

To trace the way in which a community may be corrupted, we need to explain how institutions are prevented from discharging their function as the buttresses of society. If the institutional foundations are rotten, they cannot support people in their relationships with each other. The consequence may be that some individuals can amass the resources with which to exploit others. The rent of land is the key. Cultural degradation stems, in the main, from the failure to treat rent as social revenue.

The function of each of the categories of income is a natural one. With wages, people reproduce themselves. That is to say, they labour for the means to support their families. With interest (or 'profits'), capital is reproduced. That is to say, the prospect of a reward encourages people to save part of their incomes, which can be turned into the means of production (factories, computers, screw-drivers, and so on). Rent is a community's economic surplus. As such, it is the basis of the artistic, scientific and spiritual creativity of people in association. Thus, the manner in which rent is deployed—and the manner in which the total income of society is distributed—determines the character of a society. Rent is the one source of revenue whose existence is dependent on the cooperation of all of us. And that, ironically, is the reason why it is also the most vulnerable to abuse.

Economists classify rent as a pure surplus, because it has no cost of production. This may be puzzling to those who—in the everyday but technically-loose use of the term—rent their home, or who pay commercial 'rent' for the use of offices or industrial premises. But the special significance attaching to the rents of land and natural resources is recognised in the academic literature, in which rent is classed as 'unearned'.

The exceptional nature of rent is acknowledged by those economists who identify it as the appropriate source of revenue for government. Adam Smith, for example, described rent as the "peculiarly suitable" source of revenue to defray the costs of the state.[1] That was in the 18th century. A century later, John Stuart Mill described how rents fructify even while the owner of the land is asleep, and that this growing revenue should be captured by government.[2] In the United States, what would prove to be the first global best-seller on economics at the turn into the 20th century was penned by Henry George, a San Francisco journalist who observed the formation of rent at the margins of Western settlement.[3] In Progress and Poverty his devastating critique explained why the market economy subjected people to mass unemployment in the case speculation in land was permitted.

Between them, these and other economic philosophers[4] demonstrated that there was, indeed, something unique and complex about rent. Wages, self-evidently, are the direct reward for my labour; therefore, no-one had a moral claim on that income. But who had the right to claim rent? It was, after all, a 'public value'. This was the description by Alfred Marshall, the professor of economics at the University of Cambridge whose work, a century ago, revolutionised the analytical tools employed by economists. In successive editions of Principles of Economics he worked his way towards an analysis of the role of rent in industrialised economies.

Marshall observed the way in which Britain's Parliament was locked in mortal combat as the democratically elected government fought land owners over the future of the nation's rents. Peers in the House of Lords obstructed the government's Finance Act (1909), which became known as the People's Budget. The ensuing constitutional crisis and public debate helped to clarify the social role of rent in Marshall's mind. He was originally hostile to Henry George during a lecture by the American at the University of Oxford.[5] But by the time he had polished his treatise after the First World War, Marshall settled on the view that the rent of land was, indeed, a revenue "governed by causes which are mostly beyond the control of him who determines what buildings shall be put on it".[6] He intervened to support the Liberal Government in its constitutional clash with the House of Lords in 1909. In a letter to The Times he made it emphatically clear that

The proposal made in the present Budget to isolate future accretions of 'public value' and to tax them…I regard…as in many ways a great improvement…in so far as the Budget proposes to check the appropriation of what is really public property by private persons and in so far as it proposes to bring under taxation some real income, which has escaped taxation merely because it does not appear above the surface in a money form, I regard it as sound finance. In so far as its proceeds are to be applied to social problems where a little money may do much towards raising the level of life of the people and increasing their happiness, it seems to me a Social Welfare Budget.[7]

Rent is exceptional because it originates when people engage in cooperative economic activity. Marshall and his pre-decessors understood that everyone participates in the formation of rent through the million-and-one contributions that we collectively make to the production of wealth, and to the myriad social activities that attract us to our communities.

This is not a socialist theory. A sophisticated market is required to identify, value and collect rent, with a pricing mechanism that operates within a competitive milieu. The land market performs the social function, enabling all of us to participate in the processes by which rent is creamed off the top of the economic pie. It is by this joint co-operation and competition, as individuals and as members participating in larger groups (such as private enterprises or public agencies), that we contribute towards the crystallisation of some of our output as rent. How does this knowledge, that rent is public value, help us to understanding how poverty is manufactured and culture is corrupted? We may again refer to India as an illustration.

Colonialism had to be more than a land grab. To succeed, it had to engineer a profound re-ordering of social organisation in the appropriated territories.

For the British, the primary purpose was to capture the rents generated locally for export back to London. From our theoretical exposition of rent as the source of vitality for a people's culture, we can deduce that the population suffered grievously as its public value haemorrhaged away. The scale of the losses is recorded in reports to the House of Commons based on the commercial activities of the East India Company in the second half of the 18th century.

Trade was a cover for the real intent. The British were in India to extract rent.

> Rents derived from lands constituted in those days 'the principle source of revenue.' All the lands in Bengal and Bihar were considered as belonging to the Crown or sovereign of the country, who claimed a right to collect rents or revenues from all of them.[8]

The scale of the unequal exchange is indicated by the balance of trade for the three years up to 1769. Goods and bullion worth 56.1m rupees were exported from India, offset by the import of bullion of 5.5m rupees. One of the British officials in India at the time, Richard Becher, alerted his government to the decline of the condition of the people, one consequence of which was the great famine of 1770.

The British knew that, to squeeze the rents out of such foreign territories, they had to manipulate land tenure to suit their revenue needs. This led to grievous errors of administration which inflicted terrible damage to the lives of local people.

Estates were knocked down to speculators at a revenue which…the estates were unable to bear. Ignorant of the real capabilities of the country
and incited by the hopes of profit, speculators readily agreed for sums
which were far beyond the capacity of farmers. The result was that the
districts had fallen hopelessly into arrears; and chaos invaded the entire
land revenue system.[9]

In experimenting with new ways to secure a steady flow of rents
back to Britain, the tillers of the soil were subjected to abusive
changes to land tenure. Traditional sources of authority, and related social practices, were manipulated by people who lacked
understanding of a population that had supported a once-great
civilisation. In the early decades, the tribal chiefs (zamindaris) were
made to suffer as harshly as the peasants. If they failed to pay
rents arbitrarily set at too high a level, managers were imposed
on them "who plundered the tillers of the soil and caused misery
and depopulation".[10] Where the tribal chiefs were converted into
landlords, during subsequent phases of administrative experiments, the chiefs "changed their attitude towards the tribal peas-
antry", following the shift from custom to contract.[11]

With the British government ordering new assessments on
land values (the 'Permanent Settlement'), "the landlords now got
unlimited powers of increasing the rents of the cultivators; rack-
renting ruined many families", leading to outbreaks of violence,
social chaos and confusion.[12] Concurrent with the alien legal
system introduced by the British was the conversion of tribal chiefs
to the Hindu faith.

Thus in the first half of the 19th century the traditional tribal society was
being undermined: custom was being undermined by contract, a barter
economy by a money economy they had not yet learnt to handle, and

divisions of the land determined by tribal custom were replaced by a landlord-tenant relationship.[13]

From this summary, we may perceive that the moulding of the colonial economy had little to do with the economics of the free market (which is how critics typically characterised the system, to smear 'capitalism'). It was more akin to organised brigandage. The purpose of the colonial project was the predatory acquisition of the public value through the use of force, which necessarily entailed the refashioning of people's lives—social, psychological and spiritual—in the pursuit of the appropriation and privatisation of their rents.

The Age of Colonialism

Nature exacts a charge for the use of her resources. People have to work for the benefits that they receive from her. This, generally, puts us all on a more or less equal footing. And yet, nature is blamed for cursing those communities in which people kill for her riches and corrode the institutions of civil society.

We need to explain why anti-poverty economists like Jeffrey Sachs focus so much significance on rent as an obstacle rather than a remedy. The explanation must specify why the community's surplus income—which might enrich us all—is associated with poverty on a mass scale. Marshall provides an illuminating starting point.

> These considerations lead us to repeat that, whether in an old or a new country, a far-seeing statesman will feel a greater responsibility to future generations when legislating as to land than as to other forms of wealth; and that, from the economic and from the ethical point of view, land must everywhere and always be classed as a thing by itself.[14]

Marshall affirms Adam Smith's observation that rents were the most appropriate sources of revenue to defray the costs of public goods. In feudal Europe, the king represented the state and society as the sole land owner. "Private persons were but holders subject to the obligation to work for the public wellbeing."[15] The problems began when holders decided that they would become owners. To achieve this, however, they had to erase the traditional social obligations that were attached to rent. Rent was privatised, a legal accomplishment that entailed a de facto coup against the state.

Thus, in the first phase of the Age of Colonialism, the West's own people of the commons were displaced from the acres on which they earned their living. Poverty became a defining characteristic of modernity. Many died of starvation or disease contracted in the overcrowded and unsanitary conditions in the towns and cities. Over time, millions of displaced souls were forced to sail to foreign lands, where they visited their trauma on the indigenous peoples—phase II of the colonial project.

Why did it happen? Why was rent not accorded the same proprietary safeguards as those which people applied to their wages and to the profits of their enterprises? Why was the arrogance of the land-grabbers allowed to prevail? Most of us would find agreeable a life of leisure, with the strain of having to labour for the food on our table removed by the daily flow of manna from heaven. But we recognise that this is a fantasy. It is impossible, except for those who can channel the community's rents into their pockets. That arrangement is impossible without controlling the levers of power.

Because of its public character, rent requires a framework of rules. For rent's social character can be realised only if the laws of the land protect it. There are two ways to secure its distribution, whether properly or improperly. In both cases, the state must be involved, either directly or by default.

The first way to allocate rent is through the public purse or other representative institutions through which people agree to cooperate with each other. This entails the measurement and collection of rent, and its use to fund the services that people share.

The second approach to the distribution of rent occurs by default. This happens when the state abandons its social obligations to represent everyone, and fails to allocate public value in a way that is perceived as fair to all. The consequence—in a thousand unperceived ways—is the incremental breakdown of order in civil society. The impact ranges from the acts of poverty-driven antisocial behaviour of the individual through to full-scale genocide. These are all linked by the failure of the state to exercise lawful authority on the basis of natural justice. The result is a free-for-all scramble to grab a share of the nation's rents.

- The historic roots of de-socialised rents in Europe are forgotten. But the violence that lurks in the shadows of the richest nations can, ultimately, be traced back to the breakdown of civil society as a result of the rent grab by the feudal barons.
- Warlords carve up diamond and oil resources in Africa because the state fails to secure equal opportunity for everyone. Into the void move the malevolent forces that employ destructive power to appropriate the riches of nature and create poverty.

Thus, we can see that the way in which rent is treated is the primary indicator of the character of a society. Economic historian Joseph Schumpeter alluded to this when he wrote that "nothing shows so clearly the character of a society and of a civilisation as does the fiscal policy that its political sector adopts".[16] We learn most of what we need to know about a community by examining the fiscal junction boxes. These expose the nature of power and of the rights that citizens may exercise.

Is it too late to heed Marshall's advice, that "whether in an old or a new country, a far-seeing statesman will feel a greater responsibility to future generations when legislating as to land than as to other forms of wealth"? Some social scientists, when confronted with the virtues of rent as public value, acknowledge that it should be treated as the revenue to fund the services that we share in common—but they retreat behind the claim that it is too late to make the change for 'old countries' like the United States.[17]

This excuse is no longer persuasive, because humanity has now entered a new world. In 2008, for the first time, more than half of the world's population—3.3 billion people—live in urban areas. This number will climb to 5bn over the next generation.[18] This changes the balance of our relationship with nature. UN-Habitat makes it clear that this transformation will require a "revolution in thinking". Can the displacement of most humans from their roots in the countryside become the trigger for reforms that finally abolish poverty? Or are we facing a new wave of impoverishment, this time relocated from the countryside to the town?

The evidence for this trend from China, for example, is compelling, and it illustrates how policy-makers have not yet learnt how to relate complex rights on property to optimum policies of public finance. The outcome, in China, is grievous. Despite the communist doctrine which reserves the nation's assets for the common good, large-scale corruption is being fuelled by the privatisation of resource rents.

The costs have been cautiously quantified as equal to 3% of China's economic output, or $86bn in 2003.[19] According to research by Minxin Pei, bureaucrats are stealing—on conservative assumptions—10% of land revenues, investment and government spending, and posing a "lethal threat" to China.

> A 2006 study of 3,067 corruption cases found that about half of the officials or individuals engaged in corruption related to infrastructural projects and land transactions....Typically, local officials use illegal (and sometimes violent) means to acquire farmland at low prices and later sell the user rights of the land to developers in exchange for bribes. A survey of 16 cities conducted by the Ministry of Land Resources in 2005 found that half of the land used for development was acquired illegally. According to the head of the Regulatory Enforcement Bureau at the Ministry of Land Resources, the government uncovered more than one million cases of illegal acquisition of land between 1999 and 2005.[20]

The pillaged money could fund the health and education of a population that has suffered decades of deprivation. In-stead, culture is retarded while billionaires are created in the land that still pays lip service to Marx and Mao. The richest person in China today is a 26-year-old woman, Yang Huiyan. She is reported to be worth £8.8bn following the decision of her father to list his property development company on the Hong Kong stock exchange.[21]

Legitimate money is to be made by constructing buildings that add value to China's capital stock. But much of the income gushing into the construction sector is rent that the politburo is failing to capture to fund the redevelopment of Chinese society.

De Soto: the Myth of 'Capital'

If we define corruption as the privatisation of public value, China is not far removed from the capitalist model. By its acts and omissions, it adheres to the theory that is favoured by Western financial institutions. According to their doctrine, poverty would be diminished if the neo-colonised countries privatised urban land rents: by attaching individual owners to land, and applying the rule of law, people are motivated to work and invest.

Hernando de Soto has popularised this theory in his widely acclaimed The Mystery of Capital. People who live in slums should be given secure title to their dwellings and the plots they occupy. With property deeds in their pockets, they could borrow from banks to fund new enterprises.

The shelters constructed by slum dwellers do have a value, largely because of the locations they occupy close to city centres. In Lima, Peru, for example, a house-by-house valuation (based on replacement costs in 1984) found that the average value of a slum dwelling was $22,038.[22]

If de Soto's programme was adopted, people would acquire land—most of it currently in public ownership. No doubt many of them would benefit. But what happens to the next generation of migrants from the countryside who then squat in neighbouring barrios and favelas, their dwellings constructed from scavenged materials? The crisis of poverty would be perpetuated. The de Soto formula, which was commended by politicians such as Margaret Thatcher, is based on a primitive view of property. It disregards the sophisticated layers of meaning embedded in rights that were wisely devised by pre-modern communities.

There are at least two major problems with de Soto's doctrine, in relation to his own plan to motivate people into the self-employment that would raise living standards.

First, it does not fit with reality. Fieldwork in Peru and Argentina reveals that owning the title encourages the poor to improve their homes, but they are not more likely to obtain loans from banks to start businesses. The reasons given include the belief that property is too valuable to commit as collateral, and that life's risks make people reluctant to take on debt.[23]

Secondly, the de Soto doctrine ignores how value is generated and distributed. Consequently, it ignores those public policies that can synthesise the two levels at which people live in the real world.

- Property rights need to be disaggregated into public and private categories while simultaneously harmonising them through complementary pricing mechanisms.
- The community needs to distinguish the private and public sectors, while uniting the two in an integrated community that provides everyone with the opportunity to live balanced lives.

Privatising the slums on the basis of the vulgar formula promoted by de Soto would not create the syntheses that can deliver functionally efficient communities while also safeguarding the natural environment. During the heyday of colonialism, the disasters inflicted on people and their cultures laid the foundations for the catastrophes that now loom in the 21st century. Whereas before, the predatory abuse of people's rents was a localised calamity, now they will determine the fate of humanity.

By 2050, cities are expected to support 75% of the global population. Humans are embarking on a new voyage. Our cultural future is not prescribed. On its present trajectory, that future will turn out to be the nightmare that ends all nightmares. The majority of people who will migrate from the countryside will be poor, living in squatter settlements on the edge of mega-cities. How we integrate them will determine whether we foster the conditions that nourish prosperity, or acts of terrorism and the further abuse of nature.

Generally speaking, the planners who visualise eco-friendly urban spaces have not yet understood the errors that shaped modern cities. Because of their notion of property rights and public finance, economists and sociologists continue to promote models of living that are sterile. With present thinking, the prospects remain bleak. That new strategies are not on the current agenda is affirmed by the World Bank's president, Robert Zoellick, who has promised to step up the flow of billions of dollars in extra aid. Without that foreign aid, he says, the UN's Millennium Development Goals will not be achieved.[24] In our view—recalling the failures of foreign aid over the past decades—more of the same by the World Bank will not achieve the breakthrough that is needed.

Our critique has emphasised the negative role of the West. But the neo-colonised world also needs to play its part in remedying the blight of its impoverished masses. Part 2 provides deeper scrutiny of the underlying causes of institutionalised poverty in these neo-colonial regions. Part 3 elaborates the template for solutions on the ground.

Part 2

Neo-Colonialism

4

South America:
from Farm to Favela

The Colonial Disease:
Displacement & Rent Privatisation

Of the top 20 countries with the most unequal distribution of land, 16 are in Latin America. Ewout Frankema, citing the results of the study he conducted with the World Bank, concluded that "the assertion that there is a 'Latin' type of inequality is indeed supported by a global comparison of land inequality. In Europe, countries with the most unequal distribution of land are Spain, Portugal and Italy. It is quite remarkable that land inequality in the former Iberian motherlands is as high as any in an average Latin American country".[1]

But the claim that there is a Latin American "type of inequality" may mislead. The maldistribution of land in these countries is the consequence of a general dynamic: the land grab of the past, and taxation that favours rent seekers (see box opposite). So what Latin American countries have in common with poverty stricken regions on other continents is that direct taxes (those that fall regressively harder on the poor) account for a large fraction of total government revenue. Taxes on rents of land and natural resources, on the other hand, are a small and declining fraction. Direct payroll contributions for social security, for example, represent about 18% of total tax revenue in Latin American countries. Property taxes, in contrast, represent less than 2% of overall tax revenues on average.[2] We shall trace this impact of colonialism as it evolved in Bolivia from the 16th century. There, the contours of Europe's territorial ambitions remain clear-cut today, indelibly marked on the population by spatial segregation, and by persistent high levels of income inequality.[3]

The seeds were sown by the displacement of people from land they had occupied for generations. This, in turn, delivered a captive labour force available to do the bidding of the land grabbers. In terms of life expectancy and literacy—indeed, any measure one cares to examine—Bolivia became the archetype of a country whose dynamic was the simultaneous exploitation of nature and of human beings.

It began in 1545 when the Spaniards discovered the richest silver mine in the Americas. The boom that followed enriched the settler farmers who grew maize, wheat and the coca leaf that mine workers chew to relieve hunger pains. The first model of tenure was the encomienda system, in which conquistadors received grants of land that included the rights to the labour and product of the Indians who lived on their estates. In time, this arrangement changed into the hacienda model—the extensive ownership of (largely underused) land for cattle rearing.

Bolivia became independent in 1825, but the prospects for the Indians were not improved. The white elite remained rapacious in its demands. But the country was not only gnawed away from within. It also had predators at its borders. A succession of wars

---

The Internal Colonisation of Europe

THE modern colonial project began within Europe. The feudal aristocracies, which originated as servants of monarchs (as evidenced by their status as tenants), grew tired of public service; they decided that they wanted their rewards (the rent of land) unencumbered by the duty to perform public services. So began the historic project to shear rent from the social obligations that were naturally attached to that income.

The consequences, in terms of a grossly skewed distribution of land—and so of power—are exemplified by rural Scotland. Here, according to Andy Wightman, we find today "the most concentrated, inequitable pattern of landownership anywhere in Europe".*

That Scotland was in need of land reform—or the complementary tax reform— was emphasised by Wightman's finding that "Scotland has the most concentrated pattern of private landownership in the world. Fully half of the privately-owned rural land in the country is owned by just 343 landowners".**

The model employed by the feudal aristocracy to grab the land of others (or, more precisely, the rents of others) was the model that the European powers then employed to colonise other people's territories around the world.

* Wightman (1999) ** Wightman (2001)

---

saw the country yield nearly half its territory to its neighbours.[4]

Tin was discovered in the late 19th century, fuelling a boom that doomed the remaining traditional Indian communities. The mechanism for achieving this has lessons for us today.

The government broke up free Indian communities by introducing individual titles to lands. The haciendas acquired land through small purchases in each community to break the community's cohesion, then used fraud and force as well as straight purchase to acquire Indian lands. Free communities saw their share of land fall from half in 1880 to less than a third by 1930. This third was the most unarable land.[5]

Hope was raised in 1951 with the election of Victor Paz Estenssoro as president. He nationalised the tin mines and announced a land reform. This threatened to shift resource rents into the public sector where they could fund infrastructure and raise health and literacy standards. The prospects were fabulous. Bolivia was rich in zinc, copper, silver, tungsten and gold (oil was discovered in the early 1960s). Properly directed, the resource rents could have transformed a desperately poor nation into a model for other Latin countries to emulate. But landowners had one more trick up their sleeves: the army. Suitably rewarded, the generals could be persuaded to usurp the democratic process and protect the property of the landlords.

So resumed Bolivia's long history of military coups that would go on to number 190. Factions within the army took turn to exercise dictatorial power. This consolidated the triadic partnership between the landed elites, the military and the state. The function of the state was to provide the bureaucratic channel for funnelling the resource rents from the tin mines to the elites.

The generals were well rewarded. They acquired a slice of the tin rents through the state budget, and used the army as the means to acquire land.[6] As the New York Times was to note: "Air force planes shuttle duty-free automobiles into Bolivia for officers and land titles are diverted to them at bargain prices".[7] Thus corrupted, it was a short step for the military to engage in the narcotics trade. Cocaine yielded fabulous rewards: exports to North America turned the industry into the highest earner of foreign exchange. As the price of tin on world markets declined in the 1980s, so the landowners and the military relied increasingly on a share of the coca rents.

Dramatic stories in the media conveyed the flavour of Hollywood movies such as Butch Cassidy and the Sundance Kid. Military protection provided the security for the cocaine trade. In return, the drug cartels funded coups. One such coup took place on July 17, 1980, which brought to power General Garcia Meza.[8] The occasional scandals were smoothed over and the corrupt ties reaffirmed—as occurred at a pre-coup conference involving six of the major cocaine traffickers with army leaders in La Paz on June 26, 1980. Sunday Times correspondent Nicholas Asheshov, citing reports from the us Drug Enforcement Agency, wrote: "The aim was to reach a deal allowing unrestricted growth of the coca acreage already illegally planted in Bolivia's tropical mountain jungles, plus continuation of the already lax policing of the air-freighting cocaine paste across the Amazon to Colombia and Miami".[9]

Che Guevara thought he could use Bolivia at the epicentre of a counter-revolution in Latin America. He launched his guerrilla expedition in 1967 with visions of a conquest that could spread Marxist brotherhood throughout the continent. He did not have a chance. The state—mobilised by the 'anti-communist' elites and an army flush with coca rents—was determined to preserve the privileges of its clients. Guevara became a pin-up picture on countless student dormitory walls around the world, while the rents of a rich territory were squandered in the squabbles for power. By the time democracy was restored in 1982, the colonial model was securely preserved.

"Socialism of the 21st Century"

With the reintroduction of democracy, a new phase began in Bolivia's history. Elections eventually led to the return of Victor Paz Estenssoro to the presidential palace in La Paz. He had attempted to reform property rights in 1952, and was now to be given another chance. Would he launch a new programme of reforms? A small population of under 9m people occupying a territory of more than 1m km² (nearly twice the size of France) ought to enjoy the highest material standards. They were not doing so, because the nation's land was inefficiently distributed (see box opposite).

But instead of laying the foundations for a new prosperity, Bolivia became the victim of hyper-inflation of the kind that was last seen in Germany after World War I. Following the elections in 1982, we find Jeffrey Sachs on the first of his missions, flying in to La Paz on July 9, 1985, and his first meeting with destiny.

"I did not know exactly where Bolivia was in South America," he was to record.[10] But his ignorance ran deeper. He relied for his knowledge on book learning. His speciality at Harvard was the high finance of rich nations. And yet he travelled to Bolivia to advise a government which was trapped at the bottom of the poverty league. Poverty, Sachs was to note, required a "comprehensive diagnostic checklist", which happened to be missing from his briefcase when he arrived in Bolivia. The issues that challenged that country were matters which "I had not been truly trained to address".[11] That did not inhibit Sachs from experimenting with strategies that were to evolve as shock therapy.

The academic had learnt from his history books that the way to terminate hyper-inflation was, as in Germany, sudden action to end the printing of money. The prescription worked for the monetary problems in Bolivia, and Sachs was delighted. He em-

Maldistribution of Land in Bolivia

ACCORDING to Bolivia's Agricultural Census of 1950, a tiny group of absentee landowners (4% of the population) controlled about 95% of all agricultural property, divided into units of more than 1,000 hectares each. Two-thirds of the population held under 0.25% of cultivated land in units of less than 5 hectares each (minifundia).

The Economic Commission for Latin America reported that only 21.6% of all arable lands (2% of the national territory) was under cultivation, compared to a continental average of 30%. A wide variety of forms of bondage was employed to control the peasants, including labour-duty, debt-peonage, service-tenure and share-tenure.

The process of land accumulation damaged the culture of the indigenous population. Their traditional communities (comunidades indigenas) declined from 18,000 at the beginning of the 19th century, to 3,780 by 1950. The peasants tried to fight back—there were more than 2,000 spontaneous rebellions between 1861 and 1944—but they failed. The discontent came to lead to the revolution of April 1952.*

* Source: Contemporary Archive on Latin America, London: *Fact Sheet*, July 18, 1978

ployed his model for economic 'transition' to the market economy in Poland four years later, and then again in Russia in 1990. The advice was simple:

- raise prices, especially of oil and gas, to yield government a revenue that removed the need to print the bank notes that fuelled inflation; and
- privatise state assets.

This, apparently, was the recipe that would deliver economic growth. But the monetary crisis was a symptom that reflected deep-seated problems that were beyond the understanding of the unworldly professor. President Estenssoro wanted a plan that could deliver fairness as well as efficiency; dealing with out-of-control inflation was merely one of the first steps.

William Easterly, one of Sachs' critics, attributes the hyper-inflation to "financial mismanagement" by the government, resulting in price rises that peaked at 25,000% per annum.[12] Should we not ascribe responsibility to the Bolivian government for the economic chaos? Why focus on the diagnostic shortcomings of an American scholar when the men in power in La Paz made the laws?

The problem was that, in the 1980s, democratic power came with strings attached. First and foremost, the latifundistas and their military henchmen should not be upset. So in 1985, when President Estenssoro received the proposals submitted by Sachs, he was sensitive to what had happened just 12 months earlier. Following the restoration of democracy, presidential authority was exercised by Hernán Silez Zuazo. On June 30, 1984, the president was kidnapped by the Leopards, a new narcotics police unit which had been financed and equipped by Washington to the tune of $5m. The US initiative was supposed to clamp down on the cocaine cartels. Instead, it struck against the government.[13] The attempted coup failed, however, and the president was rescued. Nevertheless, politicians were reminded of the limits of their powers.

It was the ever-present military threat that constrained democratic politics. Land reform was off limits. But that does not excuse foreign scholars who turn advisors. They are not bound by the brutal colonial legacy that shapes the political agenda in capitals like La Paz. As scientists, are they not supposed to offer optimum policies from which the politicians can choose? Sachs, by failing to understand the total problem confronting the majority in Bolivia, emphasised strategies that were piecemeal; these could not, therefore, lay the foundations for the social stability that was the precondition for sustained economic growth and an end to poverty. An example of this same shortcoming today is the emphasis Sachs now places on the need to cancel the debts of poverty-stricken countries.

Of course the colonial legacy may be approached from different angles. One of these is the debt owed to foreign financiers, which in Bolivia's case had climbed to $4.5bn in 1984, just before Sachs arrived in the country. How would this debt be addressed by anti-poverty campaigners? Today, Sachs tours the world preaching the need to cancel the debts. But what would prevent those countries from relapsing back into financial servitude? The debts were accumulated solely because home-grown rents were privatised and so were not available to fund 'public goods'. Consequently, public spending had to be funded either by taxing the poor or borrowing from the rich (usually, a combination of the two[14]). Either way, the outcome would be budgetary chaos. That insight is fundamental to any plan for stabilising an economy like Bolivia's. But this diagnosis was missing from the submission offered by Sachs to governments that welcomed him as an economic guru.

As Sachs toured the world dispensing his humanitarian charm, he (no doubt unwittingly) helped to smooth the way for IMF-framed structural reforms that usually reduced the money spent on the poor. That was to be Bolivia's fate. Twenty years after his sortie in La Paz, GDP per capita was still below the 1980 level.[15] One result was the continued exodus from the countryside as people sought urban refuge in shanty towns.

Come the millennium, South America's populist politicians—because no alternative model for growth was proposed to them—returned to socialism. It was as if the failures of the Soviet experiment had never happened. The loudest champion was President Hugo Chávez of Venezuela—proclaiming a "socialism of the 21st century". He was joined by Evo Morales, the coca farmer who was elected President of Bolivia in 2005 with the promise to nationalise the oil and gas industry. Morales secured electoral victory by campaigning against land speculation.[16] Did a model exist that could solve the problems challenging South America? Was it possible to foster the entrepreneurial economy while securing justice in the realm of land rights? If a solution existed, it had to cement town and country into a common cause. If there was one man who had the charisma and popular support to carry through such an agenda, it was Luiz Ignácio Lula da Silva.

Brazil: Cementing Town & Country

Lula, as the Brazilian president was popularly known, had a history in trade unionism. He was elected on the promise to help the poor. In the event, Brazil did enjoy economic growth, but on the back of a global boom driven by China and India's need for natural resources. It was a growth that would be terminated by the next global recession. But if he had been armed with the correct analysis of trends in the economy, Lula could have exercised his mandate to adopt those tax-and-tenure policies that would deliver sustainable growth. To achieve this, however, he would have to combine town and country into a unified strategy.

The catalyst for new strategies was to be found in the cities. Property companies flourished, as real estate prices soared into the stratosphere, but this did little to alleviate the nation's housing deficit. There was an estimated shortfall of 7.9m homes. Easy borrowing terms made mortgages accessible to the rich, but the government-owned mortgage bank (Caixa Econômica Federal) failed families on the lowest incomes. Slums continued to blight the inner cities where high-value activities co-existed with marginalised sections of the population.

Housing policy in the neo-colonial era requires the demolition of slums to make way for expensive properties, leaving the poor to relocate in whatever crevices they can find elsewhere. The alternative strategy is a redesigned tax system that attracts the rents of land into the public purse. This yields the self-funding approach to capital formation that avoids becoming indebted to international financiers. But on this the consensus in Washington is silent (see box over).

How would investment in infrastructure drive Brazil on to a new growth path? One answer is provided by the solution to the problem that confronted farmers. Despite their success at increasing crop yields, Brazil's farmers were unable to compete on the international markets because of the costs of transportation. They were disadvantaged by a pitiful highway network. It cost $80 per tonne to deliver grain to coastal ports, twice the cost faced by Argentina's farmers and four times the cost carried by United States farmers.[17]

What would happen if Brazil's transport costs were slashed from $80 to $20? Under the current tax regime, land owners would raise their rents. But what if government shifted to a funding arrangement that recycled back into the public purse the rents that flowed from public investment in a new highway network? The additional revenue—created by the roads—would fund the capital costs of that infrastructure. So the new investment would not be a financial burden on anybody's earned incomes.

Now relate this fiscal model to the urban context. If slum-dwellers are to be rehoused on low-value land on the city fringe, government is faced with providing roads and sewerage systems as well as schools and hospitals. Under the current tax regime, the funds for these services are not available. That is why the dwellers of the favelas and barrios are left to fend for themselves. Why should we be surprised if some of them resort to gangsterism?

The self-funding model—where the infrastructure pays for itself—however, removes the financial obstacle to investment in 'public goods'. As government invests in the roads and the schools that families need, so the rents of land in the new catchment areas rise to pay for these services. This virtuous circle automatically generates the employment opportunities that people need, with an affordable rise in wages.

This model of tenure-and-taxation, we shall see (in Part 3), ends spatial segregation. It was the model of development that Western advisors failed to place on Lula's desk. Reforming politicians continue to be hampered by the void in vital statistics. The prospects look bleak in Latin America, but all was not lost for the neo-colonised world. The Anglo-colonial legacy offered some hope in Asia.

The Information Void

THE World Bank confirms that the colonial heritage underpins the persistent high levels of inequality in Latin American countries. And yet, the Bank persists with policies that neither redistribute land itself nor, alternatively, shares the revenue from land equitably.

Tax-and-tenure reform is hindered by the paucity of data on land values and their distribution. The international financial institutions which actively prescribe profound social change do not deploy similar enthusiasm for collating data on land. Governments are encouraged to adopt revenue-raising instruments favoured by the World Bank and the IMF.

The information void favours those conditions that determined the kind of appropriation that was imposed on South America.

In areas with unfavourable settler conditions, colonists adhered to a type of rent seeking behaviour that may have suppressed the rural economy as a whole due to the burden of taxes, but did not affect the existing distribution of land. The redistribution of land from natives to colonists was part of a colonial policy with extractive and developmental objectives. The expropriation of land and the exploitation of forced labour served extractive purposes, but investments in the local economy in order to raise the profitability of agricultural production served developmental purposes.*

The tragedy remains that, post-independence, governments continue to neglect the information about land and rents even as some of their leaders launch polemical attacks on imperial powers of the past. So governments that claim to be speaking for the poor continue to use tax tools that penalise that constituency, while persisting with policies that favour the elite rich.

* Frankema (2006) p. 7

5

Asia: the Role of Mega-Projects

The Capitalist Disease: Infrastructure's Windfalls

Every society needs capital-and-culture-intensive infrastructure that supports its population. Private enterprise in the modern economy could not survive without those public goods. Entrepreneurs need the back-up of services ranging from public health to the rule of law. But in the competitive market, a feed-back mechanism is at work which subverts the intended outcomes of these shared services.

Competition delivers optimum efficiency only if the distribution of income also conforms to the principles of justice. By this, we mean that the value generated by the producers of goods and services should be shared by those who engage in its production. Trouble starts when part of the value leaks into the hands of those whom we elsewhere designate 'Predators'.[1]

In the capitalist economy, most social and economic problems stem from the fact that the pricing mechanism is legally and institutionally constrained from functioning either efficiently or fairly. Specifically, the problem is located in the system of public prices—government's taxes—which are a covert way of redistributing income from the poor to the rich. This is how it happens: everyone pays taxes when goods and services are consumed, when transactions in the capital markets are undertaken, or when wages and salaries are earned. That tax revenue is pooled by government and much of it is used to fund infrastructure and services which raise the productivity of the economy. This ought to be good news for everyone. In fact, it is bad news, because the net gains are crystallised into land values. This part of economic value, created by society's progress, is taken by the owners of land, including home-owners. So everyone's taxes, including those of the poor who do not own their homes or other land, are used to create value which is captured by the relatively rich, who own land, for the most part under their houses. In other words, the wealthy effectively receive back the money they pay in taxes.[2]

- If land values—as annual flows of rent—were recycled back into the public purse, they would fund the infrastructure needed to operate an efficient economy and a fair society.
- If land values are privately appropriated, they cannot be consumed or invested by the community. This obliges people who work for their living to pay taxes to fund the infrastructure that profits the landowners.

In the latter case the principle of fairness is abused by government. But people are also burdened with taxes that damage the incentives to work, save and invest in productive enterprises. This maldistribution from low income earners to high income asset owners has been documented for the UK.[3]

The lessons for neo-colonised countries are vital. The scale of the challenges they face today are magnified far beyond anything that confronted governments in Europe at the dawn of the Industrial Revolution (see box below). But the opportunities are also enormous—if the problems are converted by good governance into capital formation at an accelerated pace.

Triple Whammy

THE Asia-Pacific region is experiencing the triple dynamics of economic growth, urbanisation and poverty. It accounts for 34% of the global urban population, and is home to over 40% of slum dwellers. India has nearly 62m people living in slums and squatter settlements.*

* Kumari Selja, India's Minister of Housing and Urban Poverty Alleviation (December 15, 2006)

The construction industry, for example, could play a leading role in speeding up economic growth within a balanced social framework. The extent of the need for new dwellings in Asia is difficult to grasp. India alone will need 24m more homes over the next decade. But whether builders can contribute to net gains from capital formation and consumer satisfaction depends on the kind of pricing mechanism that is employed to deliver growth.

At present, the prospects are not good. The Indian government (in 2008) is committed to a Washington Consensus-based strategy which emphasises foreign investment in real estate, and the formation of "secondary mortgage markets and securitisation and pro-poor partnerships where 10-15% of land is earmarked for providing 20-25% dwellings for the poor".[4] This is the confused conflation of Welfare State with the de Soto model of property rights.

The financial model on which India is basing its hopes will perpetuate the boom/busts that are endemic in the capitalist economy.[5] But the people of India cannot afford to lose time or waste resources on avoidable recessions. For all her vaunted achievements in recent years, "in 2003 there were hardly 5m workers in organised manufacturing out of a labour force of over 350m!"[6]

Asia could drive her economies to new plateaux of sustainable growth by making infrastructure available to the majority of the urbanised population who live in the smaller towns and cities. The challenge is to halt the exodus of capital resources, which "tend to seek the better infrastructure of existing large cities".[7] There is one way only to prevent this exodus: remove the attractions of windfall gains from land, which are larger in the mega-cities. This (as we explain in Part 3) would create the 'level playing field' between people, so that lopsided development is avoided.

China is the one country in Asia that has retained the opportunity to accomplish this by applying in a consistent way the rules of the market economy. Will the Communist Party, which has not had its power wrested from it by a Yeltsin, learn the secrets of inclusive prosperity? Or will it hand the nation's natural riches to their version of the Russian oligarchs?

China: the Teachings of Dr. Sun

Jeffrey Sachs arrived in China in 1992. He found that the Communist Party had retained its grip on the political process over the previous 20 years, and was not willing to be beguiled by

Western doctrines.

China had experimented with ways to embrace market mechanisms for producing wealth without abandoning socialist sentiments. How sincere the Maoist doctrine was in relation to the values of equality and brotherhood (millions died during the Cultural Revolution) is for history to determine. But the politburo that was engineering change was cautious.

That did not inhibit Jeffrey Sachs. He launched himself into regular visits as an advisor to economic scholars who had been educated in the West. He graduated to advisor to senior government officials on issues like the development of remote Western provinces. China needed a model of development, but did it need advice that had helped to catapult Russia into economic and social disaster? Could she draw on home-grown lessons that identified ways to establish an efficient market economy that was fair to everyone?

The foundations of such a philosophy were laid by Sun Yat-Sen (1866-1925). He led the revolutionary Kuomintang forces that overthrew the Manchus, the last imperial dynasty. His manifesto, San Min Chu I ('Three Principles of the People'), distilled classical economic science from the West with the ancient wisdom of China (see box over).

One of the key planks of Dr. Sun's reform was to combine land tenure with a public finance system that drew its revenue from rent. This could be achieved if the state enacted two regulations: "First, that it will collect taxes according to the declared value (by land-owners) of the land; second that it can also buy the land at the same price". Dr. Sun's formula trapped the land owners. If they under-assessed the value of their land, to reduce their tax liability, the state could purchase their property for what would be less than its market price.

When asked by American reporters for the origins of his fiscal philosophy, Dr. Sun replied: "The teaching of your single taxer, Henry George, will be the basis of our programme of reform. The land tax as the only means of supporting the government is an infinitely just, reasonable, and equitably distributed tax".[8]

Dr. Sun pursued the policy to its logical conclusion, advocating that "after land values have been fixed, we should have a regulation by law that from that year on, all increases in land values...shall revert to the community". This was the strategy commended by John Stuart Mill, who proposed to leave existing rents with their owners. Eventually, rents would grow to the point where it would not be necessary to tax labour and capital. This policy would have launched China on the road to prosperity without the need for the traumatic experiment in communism.[9]

But if the lessons of the pre-Mao home-grown philosophy needed to be complemented, the Politburo in present-day Beijing could draw on the example of Taiwan. Here was a Chinese people who, out of necessity, developed a strategy that delivered prosperity and the prototype for a new player on the global scene—the Asian Tiger. The people who had followed General Chiang Kai-shek into exile on Formosa took with them the teachings of their first leader, Dr. Sun Yat-Sen.

The Statute for the Equalisation of Urban Land Rights was enacted in 1954 to complement the land-to-the-tiller policy. Chiang's government structured its compensation to landlords so that the latter were obliged to invest their money in urban industrial enterprises. In addition, government raised a significant portion of state revenue from the rent of land. These policies laid the foundations from which Taiwan's take-off was launched. Further measures, such as the Land Tax Law (1977), provided

Three Principles of the People

DR. SUN combined the principle that "each tiller of the soil shall possess his own fields" with the modernising need for capital investment and the scientific rotation of crops.* In 1924, Dr. Sun's Kuomintang political party fleshed out the detail of its plan to reduce the share of rents taken by landlords and to consolidate the rights of tenant farmers.** In the industrial sector, the Kuomintang manifesto pledged to promulgate laws to elevate the status of industrial workers, including the creation of factory councils to facilitate consultation between employers and employees—the model of works councils that were so successful in Germany after World War II.

Mao's Communist Party, which ultimately vanquished the Kuomintang, acknowledged San Min Chu I but favoured the economics of Das Kapital. At the Communist Party's 17th Party Congress in 2007, however, President Hu Jintao conceded that Mao's theory of class struggle was erroneous; but offered no insight into the errors in the hybrid model which they were developing, which attempts to merge communism with capitalism.

The modern Chinese model is enriching the few in the same way as has occurred in capitalist countries, for the same reason—the failure to treat rent as public revenue. Thus, Hu's doctrine—"To realise social equity and justice is the Chinese Communists' consistent position"—was contradicted by the emergence of 106 billionaires in China in 2007, a leap from just one such rich person in 2003,† while peasants in the countryside rioted in protest against state-sponsored land grabs.

* Yat Sen (1929) pp. 456-464   ** Tawney (1932) p. 83, n.1   † Sheridan (2007)

The Opportunity Cost of the Command Economy		
	People's Republic of China	Taiwan
GDP (PPP) per capita ($)	5,896	27,600*
Unemployment (%)	9.9	4.4
Government spending (% of GDP)	20.8	15.3
Top Income Tax Rate (%)	45	40
Top Corporate Tax Rate (%)	33	25

Source: Kane, Holmes and O'Grady (2007)
* 2005 (purchasing power parity)

stronger regulatory and enforcement powers for land-related charges.

The above table compares some of the vital statistics of the two Chinas. Suitably interpreted, it might lay the basis for a counter-factual history. What if, instead of choosing the command economy prescribed by Marx, Chairman Mao had adopted Dr. Sun's doctrines in 1949 (the year he drove Chiang's nationalists from the mainland)? The difference between the countries in per capita GDP gives us a sense of the wealth that was denied the people of the mainland. If the warlords had desisted; if Mao had resisted Marx's theory of the inevitability of socialism; if Dr. Sun's programme had been institute—since 1949, the people of China would have enjoyed material prosperity on a wondrous scale.[10]

But Beijing could also draw on the lessons from Hong Kong—the single most successful market economy in the free world. (Hong Kong is reviewed in chapter 8.) Its fiscal philosophy sympathetically reflected the norms of social solidarity and individual prosperity that were supposed to be at the heart of Marxist ideology. Thus, the overwhelming evidence, from Sun's teachings and the records of Taiwan and Hong Kong, directs attention to the one issue that was curiously absent from the teachings of Jeffrey Sachs: the need to locate the tenure-and-tax nexus at the heart of any strategy for transforming the socialist economy, or for eliminating poverty.

During the early 1990s, Sachs observed the trends that were to lead up to the passage of China's Real Rights Law in 2007, and he examined Western interpretations of China's model. He noted that the commune system in agriculture was dismantled in favour of incentives to farmers to increase their output. "This was shock therapy par excellence," he gleefully noted.[11] Peasants were also freed to move into the towns where capital could be invested for private profit. Enterprise zones were designated which provided tax incentives to investors.

> The rest, as they say, is history. These zones took off. They combined very low-cost labour, availability of international technology, and an increasing and eventual torrent of investment funds, both from domestic savings, but increasingly in the 1990s, foreign direct investment.[12]

Sachs does not identify the flaw in this model. The evidence was abundantly available in Britain and the United States, where enterprise zones were deployed by the Thatcher and Reagan administrations. The result was disproportionate rewards for land owners, who pocketed the tax incentives that were supposed to reward investors who created jobs. In other words, enterprise zones were one example of a generic process in which rent-seekers drain the economy of the surplus for their private benefit, at the expense of everyone else.

In China, the result was unintended: people who occupied land in the coastal ports were able to privatise the rents because the state failed to collect this revenue to fund public services. In 2007, while GDP grew at an annual rate of almost 12%, government struggled to control inflation driven by the property sector.

China's market-based achievements were impressive. In the 20 years to 2001, 400m people were elevated out of poverty. But by allowing rental income to be privatised by default she is storing up the deep-seated problems which in the past have led to violent social upheavals.

Progress against absolute poverty began to slow in the latter half of the 1990s. Having swapped Marx for the market, the communists were exposed to the capitalist disease which creates a permanent class of outcasts.

Nevertheless, the Communist Party's institutional approach to the mixed political-and-economic model preserved the opportunity to push reforms further in the direction of Dr. Sun than Dr. Sachs. In 2007, the National People's Congress passed the Real Rights Law. Western commentators emphasised the legal protection for private property. The law did, indeed, affirm the private ownership of goods and man-made capital. But it resolutely affirmed that land and nature's resources would remain in the public domain. Individuals were free to hold secure land-use rights. Fatally, however, the law failed to enshrine the reciprocal of that legal right, namely, the obligation to pay the market rent into the public purse. One consequence was the incentive to corruption by state officials. In 2006, over 8,300 party members were punished for accepting bribes.[13]

Statecraft and Social Funding

There is not a corner of Asia that has not been torn by post-colonial Marxist-inspired conflict. The command economy has now been abandoned, and good riddance to it, according to Jeffrey Sachs. The central state has outlived its usefulness, he tells us.

> Why? China's centralised apparatus, which extends over such a large area, is not compatible with the dynamism of a decentralised and diverse market economy and market-based society, which depends on migration, multiple bases of power and wealth, and regional diversity. This dynamism is already putting huge strains on Chinese statecraft.[14]

A new model of statecraft was needed compatible with the logic of markets. But an incomplete model was offered to his audiences in China when Sachs lectured them on the need to empower provincial and local governments. Experiment was needed that allowed for "diversity, creating a more complex division of labour, and enabling mobility—in short, to see what works".[15]

But there was no need for China's administrators to re-invent the wheel. We know what does not work in the market economy; and that optimum results are achieved when the pricing mechanism distinguishes rent from the wages of labour and the profits of capital. This model was not elaborated by Sachs, which is why we do not share his optimism that China would "end poverty in the 21st century".[16] Neither Britain nor the United States has terminated poverty despite two centuries of market-based growth. Why should China succeed where they have failed?

But China—indeed, the rest of Asia—could abolish poverty by employing the statecraft that synchronises good governance with the rules that motivate people in the productive economy. The scale of the challenges are enormous, but they could be turned into solutions if the people were liberated to work in communities that excluded the exploitation by the rent-seekers. The state has a crucial role to play as a partner with the people in the provision of infrastructure. From international highway networks for the millions who will migrate into cities in the next few decades (and will need new homes), to the renewal of water and sewerage systems—they all require the commitment of vast resources. Those resources would be generated by the infrastructural services themselves. The success with which Asia drives her economies to prosperity on the back of such mega-projects depends entirely on what happens to the gains from these investments.

Infrastructure need not be a financial burden on anyone. It offers self-funding opportunities for raising the quality of the lives of everyone. The author has described the technical terms for this funding process in Wheels of Fortune.[17]

So Asian governments need not depend on foreign financial institutions for the money to initiate the projects that would deliver economies of scale and accelerate the redevelopment of low income countries. By declaring in advance that the infrastructure would be funded out of the rents which they created, bankers, including those in the West, would be aware that the projects were viable ('white elephant' investments are excluded from this category). Those bankers would be willing to provide funding, even though rents would be beyond their reach. Western technical expertise and capital would be subordinated to the common good of host countries.

Once the principle of who-gets-what is clarified, the pricing mechanism would take care of the practical problem of dividing rents from the share that goes to labour and capital. This funding model is compatible with the devolution of decision-making, so that people may express their preferences on what meets their needs. In fact, it is only when people-power is released at the local level that the maximum rents can be generated. In other words, the financial viability of an infrastructure project is contingent on

6

Africa: the Great Plunder

The Constitutional Disease:
South Africa & the Wealth Gap

Post-apartheid South Africa's new constitution was written while the African National Congress (ANC) was in power and Nelson Mandela was president. The constitution was the outcome of extensive public consultation. Grassroots participation in the formulation of the document was so intensive that the people could fairly claim to own the principles contained in it.

During its freedom-fighting days, the ANC adopted the principle (in its 1955 Freedom Charter), that "the land shall be shared among those who work it". The constitution reflected the spirit of this ideal by declaring that the land of South Africa belonged to all of its people. There is no clause in it which qualifies this statement in favour of a minority. But missing from the constitution was the clause that identified the rents of land as belonging to the nation. This omission would be the cause of the failure to unite the races in the common cause—peace and prosperity for everyone.

A decade after the end of apartheid, on June 24, 2003, landless people marched on Parliament to voice their frustration at the rate at which land was being made available to them. The ANC government had adopted the formula of restitution based on the principle that the market price would be paid for land relinquished by white farmers for the benefit of the landless. It was calculated that, under the budgeted proposals, it would actually take 96 years to achieve the five-year target that had been adopted—in the reconstruction programme that began in 1994—of redistributing 30% of farmland.[1]

The constitutional provision was meaningless for millions of people who were unable to till the soil. But in July 2007 the Department of Land Affairs announced that it was confident that the land restitution target set for 2008 would be achieved. There was, however, one problem: the steep increase in the price of land. That was why the government was anxious to accelerate restitution, to beat future increases in land prices. This tension between land rights and land prices illustrates the incompleteness of approaching tenure separately from taxation. Without integrating the two, the inevitable outcome is the continued migration of displaced people to the towns where they end up in slums searching for informal ways to keep themselves alive.

This problem is illustrated by Botswana, whose philosophy of tenure we acknowledged as remarkable (chapter 2). But despite the land rights provisions in its constitution, Botswana also experiences the migration of people out of the countryside. Slums have emerged around the towns, and in one notorious case the authorities demolished the dwellings of squatters who were deemed to be illegal occupants. The squatters could not afford the high rents in the capital, Gaborone, so they occupied communal land in Mogoditshane. Such an outcome is inevitable, if society does not balance its revenue-raising system with its land laws (see box).

Neo-Colonialism and Spatial Encroachment

URBAN policy in neo-colonised countries displaces people beyond the areas of high land value to where they lack the infrastructure that is essential for high-density living.

Although governments consider themselves independent of their former colonial masters, spatial segregation—a defining characteristic of urban colonialism—ensures that the policies of the past prevail in the present. This irony has been noted by scholars.

- Bangalore, in India, has experienced "extensive evictions and demolitions of settlements, especially small business clusters in productive urban locations. The demolished land is reallocated by master planning to higher income interest groups, including corporations".

- Mike Davis, an urban sociologist, notes that "post-colonial elites have inherited and greedily reproduced the physical footprints of segregated colonial cities. Despite the rhetoric of national liberation and social justice, they have aggressively adapted the racial zoning of the colonial period to defend their own class privileges and spatial exclusivity".

Despite paying lip service to equality, laws protect property rights so that urban segregation may be likened to social warfare. Spatial boundaries are continually redrawn for the benefit of land owners. Examples of this process in the West range from Baron Haussmann's redevelopment of Paris in the 1860s to Margaret Thatcher's redevelopment of London's Docklands in the 1980s.

* Benjamin (2001) p. 4 ** Davis (2006)

But for policy-makers, the tax-and-tenure model requires them to understand how the market distributes income. Without that understanding, Africa will continue to be a nation plundered. A tragic example is offered by Zimbabwe.

Zimbabwe: Operation Clear Out the Trash

Robert Mugabe wanted to steer a new course for his people. When white Rhodesians capitulated and agreed to a con-stitutional settlement, transferring political power to the black majority, a new era began. Or did it? They re-named the country Zimbabwe, and the capital became Harare. But would this post-colonial phase of Britain's ex-possession lead to a new prosperity for the people who had been dispossessed of their land?

Independence was sealed with signatures in 1979, at a conference in London. The Lancaster House Agreement set the terms for the rights that would be respected by the political parties. The West was satisfied with the settlement, and Mugabe was elected the first Prime Minister. There had been one major obstacle to the settlement: disagreement on land reform. But Mugabe was pressured to sign. The British and US governments offered to buy land from white farmers for allocation to landless peasants. At that point the whites, who made up 1% of the population, owned 70% of the most fertile land.

The first phase of redistribution in the 1980s was funded in part by the UK. About 70,000 people were settled on 20,000 square kilometres of land. The unfolding events received the United Nations' seal of approval in 1994 for what it called "an impressive record on social integration". In its Human Development Report, the UN stated:

> After independence, the government reassured the whites that their
> property would be respected. But it also concentrated public investment
> on basic social services—which directed resources to the poorer black
> community.[2]

What could go wrong? At the constitutional conference,
Mugabe and his 'terrorists' had signed a treaty agreeing to end
their civil war by not expropriating white farms. Furthermore, he
honoured the undertaking to put whites in strategic government
positions—including Minister of Agriculture and Minister of
Commerce and Industry.

> These measures reassured the white community that it was
> welcome to remain if it was willing to work within the new
> democratic framework.[3]

There was, however, one slight problem with this arrangement.
The UN noted that the guarantees enjoyed by the whites "also
perpetuated considerable inequality. They still own almost half
the land and nearly all the investment capital in mining and
industry". The UN added: "Although there has been no direct
redistribution of land or other resources, the government has given
priority in social spending to the communal lands that are home
to most of the black community".[4] The black leaders honoured
their deal with the whites, but unemployment rose. Private
investment fell as a proportion of GDP. A crisis was growing, and
the international financial experts would have to be consulted.

In 1991, Zimbabwe accepted the IMF's structural adjustment
programme, a classic example of the Washington Consensus in

action. It was to devastate the lives of the poor.

- The government was obliged to re-introduce school fees. Predictably, children of low income families were with-drawn from school.
- Health care charges were imposed on the poor.
- Infant mortality rates began to rise.

This was a bitter price to pay for political independence. Democracy had arrived, but the black population discovered that little had changed on the home front. Still, reported the UN,

> Zimbabwe has made remarkable progress in social integration. Its major achievement lies in raising the human development levels of the black community without restricting opportunities for the white population— thus avoiding social tension.[5]

But the aspirations of the indigenous population were not being fulfilled. Mugabe tried it the British way and he tried it the IMF way, and both ways failed.[6] What was he to do now in response to the public demand for improved education and health for all the children of Zimbabwe? No constructive model of change was on offer that would make long-term sense to both black and white. One man who knew why, from the inside, was the former chief economist at the World Bank. Joseph Stiglitz understood the reasons why, in these situations, the recommendations coming out of Washington excluded proposals for land reform. He wrote: "Taxation, and its adverse effects, are on the agenda: land reform is off....[L]and reform represents a fundamental change in the structure of society, one that those in the elite that populates the finance ministries, those with whom the international financial institutions interact, do not necessarily like".[7]

Mugabe, like a cornered animal, lashed out. The key was the land that had earned for Zimbabwe the accolade of being one of Africa's bread baskets. The Zanu-PF government decided that land would have to be expropriated from white owners. Thus began a land grab that had nothing to do with either economic efficiency or justice. Some of the most fertile farms were acquired by Mugabe's supporters, then not put to use, and the population began to starve.

Mugabe turned into a tyrant. Now, after the whites had fled the country, he turned on his own people. He launched one of the most disgraceful episodes in neo-colonial history. The dwellers of the slums in Harare were subjected to terror as the police demolished their shacks and expelled the dwellers from the city. Their president called it Operation Clear Out the Trash. The slums were emptied with as much ceremony as people emptying their trash cans.

By 2007, hundreds of thousands of people were suffering a humanitarian crisis. Mugabe had claimed the government would build homes for the slum dwellers, but the rehousing programme provided dwellings for 3,300 families out of an evicted population estimated at between 700,000 and 1m people.[8] More than a quarter of the country's population fled Zimbabwe—about 3.4m people. Those that remained struggled to squeeze food out of the neglected soil. About 80% of able-bodied people were unemployed, and life expectancy was reduced to the lowest in the world.

Might it have been different? When the time came for "fundamental economic change", as the UN put it, could the government have settled for a tax-led land reform? What if, instead of grabbing the land, the government had merely required farmers—black and white—to pay the rental value of their land into the public purse? And what if it offset this new source of revenue with corresponding cancellation of taxes on the wages of people—black and white—and on the profits from capital investment? Would this have encouraged people to grow more food? To invest more capital on the land? To attract foreign investors who would know that, by adding to the nation's income, they would enjoy tax-free profits?

Some white farmers would have complained that the charges on rents were a confiscation, but they would still possess the title deeds. And they would not be paying more than the costs of the public services they were using. In other words, they would be paying for the benefits they received—as they willingly did when they purchased a combine harvester from a manufacturer or fertilisers from a chemical company. The principle is exactly the same when buying services from a public agency, to use public highways, enjoy the benefits of civil administration and police protection for property. This outcome would have been superior to the tragedy that befell Zimbabwe because of the absence of a sustainable programme of reforms that would deliver prosperity for everyone.

Post-independence, the extra rents which were created were significant, and they were available for investment in Zimbabwe's future (see box facing). But nobody told Robert Mugabe that this strategy was a viable option. He was kept in the dark by the IMF and the World Bank, which were well aware of this variant of 'structural reform'. They did not recommend the policy because it would confine the rents within Zimbabwe for the benefit of the whole population. The price of silence was that everyone lost—black and white. One measure of that loss is indicated by the collapse in exports. Just before the land grab began, commercial farmers earned US$800m,

52% of Zimbabwe's export earnings. In 2007, that revenue had plunged to US$4m.

As the rate of death of hungry children accelerated, government ministers began to confess. Agriculture Minister Rugare Gumbo blamed the food shortages on black farmers who had taken over formerly white-owned land. He pointed to the theft of stock and irrigation equipment and the vandalism of infrastructure by the new farmers, as well as the underuse of land. Despite this record,

---

Pocketing the Peace Dividend

IN times of trouble, the decline in the economy's productivity is immediately registered in the property market. Land values drop. With peace, they rise.

When Wilf Mbanga bought his home in Harare in 1980, he paid the equivalent of £23,000 sterling. As founder of The Daily News, he tracked the evolving post-colonial history. This brought him into conflict with the Mugabe government. When his newspaper was closed down in 2003, he went into exile in Britain. From Hythe, on the Kent coast, where he published The Zimbabwean, he was informed in 2007 by his insurance company that the property back home would have been worth £500,000. But in the market place, the Mugabe effect had reduced its value to £300,000.

Lonrho, with its history as an African mining conglomerate, knew that the peace dividend—following the demise of Mugabe's regime—would be appreciable. It established a £100m fund to invest in Zimbabwe's commercial property and infrastructure. Purchasers would benefit by buying real estate while it was cheap. But that would all change.

"As the economy does start to grow significantly, hotels are going to be one of the first big kick-off areas. There are some pretty under-valued properties in Zimbabwe at the moment," according to David Lenigas, the Executive Chairman of Lonrho.*

* Pfeifer (2007)

---

however, Mugabe pressed on with the displacement of white farmers as the October 2007 deadline for their removal arrived.[9]

Zimbabwe, a nation that could have helped to feed the hungry of Africa, became a state relying on private welfare—including the us$500m a year in remittances that flowed into the country from exiled Zimbabweans in South Africa.

The tragedy of this one country, however, was a metaphor for its continent's woes. As a measure of what Africa as a whole was losing, in 1990, according to one estimate, 40% of the continent's wealth was held abroad. Today for each dollar of aid that goes into Africa, at least five dollars flows out 'under the table' to tax havens such as Britain's Channel Islands, according to a former economic advisor to Jersey.[10] Most of that foot-loose money is the rent of the continent's natural resources.

In 2007, reports began to circulate that South Africa—acting as honest broker between Mugabe and the opposition—would propose reforms to the constitution. Did the country that had successfully abolished apartheid have the remedy for landlessness?

We have seen that there are reasons to doubt Pretoria's qualifications to offer advice to its neighbour. But we return to this issue in chapter 9, where we suggest that South Africa could be a pioneer for prosperity.

Nigeria:
Oiling the Wheels of Corruption

Evidence for the mechanism that institutionalises corruption as a social process is to be found beneath our feet. All the information we need is strewn on the pavements of our cities. The anatomy of corruption in the making may be perceived as we go about our daily business. We shall recount one example.

Our story begins in Nyevsky Prospekt, the Fifth Avenue of St. Petersburg. Here, out of the ashes of Soviet communism, emerged the entrepreneurs ready to use what space they could find. The people could not wait for Russia to develop a commercial property market to accommodate retailers. Kiosks sprang up on the pavements. Traders came from Azerbaijan and Tajikistan to sell to a public that was hungry for their wares. From exotic regions of the east the spirit of the free market flowed in and ended up as deals outside the Metros of Moscow and the gates of the walled city of Novgorod.

Municipal governments, including St. Petersburg, issued licenses for the kiosks, and charged a few roubles as rent. Then came the mafia. They wanted 'protection money' from the traders. It might be wondered how the entrepreneurs could afford to pay. The answer was to be found in the locations occupied by the kiosks. Traders situated closest to Metro station entrances had the highest turnover. They paid the flat fee to the municipal government, but paid much higher sums to the mafia. Kiosks further along the highway, where the pedestrian footfall was lower, paid smaller sums for 'protection'.

Nobody taught the mafia and the kiosk traders about David Ricardo's theory of rent.[11] But this was the marketplace: the better the location, the higher the rent that the tradesmen were willing to pay. They could pay, and they did pay. The problem was that the money went to the bullies waiting to grab it.

The lesson is this: if government does not charge the full market rent for the benefits derived from a public space, the difference is not vaporised: it is privatised. In this case, hoodlums realised that there was spare cash on the pavements of Nyevsky Prospekt waiting to be picked up and pocketed. As for the traders, they settled for the easy life: it was all the same to them who collected the rents as long as they were free to transact their business and retain their wages and the profits from the sale of their stock.

The same reality exists on the pavements of India's cities. Migrants from the countryside stake out a few square metres and erect flimsy shacks which they call home. They choose locations close to where they can find work. Pedestrians are displaced on to the highways. The slum dwellers can and do pay the rents of these locations. But because the rents are not collected by the local government, the dadas—the local goons—pocket the money in return for 'protection'.

Here, then, is the choice offered by the market economy. Competition equalises the returns to labour and capital. Because wages and profits are privately earned, their owners make sure they claim what is due to them. But rent is public value. If the stewards of the community's interests fail to collect that revenue, others have no scruples about appropriating what is not theirs. Corruption as an institutionalised process originates with the failure of governance. In Africa, the losses are enormous. Nigeria bears witness to the fact that the poverty of that continent cannot be attributed to the malevolence of nature.

Over 90% of Nigeria's population live on less than $2 a day, while civil conflicts are fuelled by the oil rents which government fails to collect for the public's benefit. Corruption pervades individual deeds, corporate strategies and government policies. From terrorist attacks by malcontents, to bribes paid into Swiss bank accounts and vote rigging at elections, all can be traced back to the failure of public policy in relation to oil rents.

Campaigners against oil-fuelled corruption argue that

transparency in all deals involving rent would mitigate the damage. That is why Tony Blair, when Britain's Prime Minister, initiated the Extractive Industries Transparency Initiative (EITI). But the trouble is that the temptations are affordable, if the costs of corruption can be funded out of rent.

> Even companies that would rather not pay bribes may feel compelled to as the price of access to that country. Competition between companies is thus no longer based on merit, but on the ability of a company to pay higher awards to well-connected public officials than its competitors: this is a situation which naturally favours more unscrupulous companies.[12]

The sums are huge. In one case in 2007, a US conglomerate (which was a subsidiary of Halliburton) was under investi-gation. It was alleged that it was paying $170m in bribes for a natural gas contract in Nigeria. This corruption sprawls by osmosis.

Audited disclosure of resource rental payments is crucial for enhancing performance of the market economy, but it is not sufficient to eliminate corrupt behaviour (see box below). The only way to remove corruption—in both its legal and extra-legal forms—is for resource rents to be drawn into the public purse for the benefit of everyone. Will Africa be able to separate rent privatisation from the interests of the political elites who now exploit the continent's natural resources?

Models of good governance do exist which can guide govern-ments that want to serve the common good. One is to be found in Alaska, where oil rents are collected for the future welfare of every state citizen. In addition, every eligible resident receives an annual dividend as high as $2,000.[13]

Sach's Doctrine of the Resource Curse is nonsense. Nature's resources do not curse anyone. Rather, the curse flows from bad stewardship of the public domain.

Good Governance: A Princely Price

AN example of how governments conspire to enter into contracts that are apparently transparent but involve questionable payments is the £1bn disbursed by Britain under a weapons contract.

The government of Saudi Arabia paid £43bn out of its oil rents to a British firm, BAE, which in turn paid £30m a quarter, over 10 years, to a Saudi prince. Was this a corrupt deal? No, said the prince, who could honestly demonstrate that the payments to the bank account which he controlled in New York were sanctioned by both the British and Saudi governments. But the facts could not be tested in a British court, because the Serious Fraud Office investigation was terminated, reportedly under pressure from Prime Minister Tony Blair and the Attorney General, on the grounds that a prosecution would jeopardise Britain's national security.*

*Leigh and Evans (2007)

Part 3

The Economics of Abundance

7

Governance & the UN

"A High Political Price"

Economics, if applied scientifically, leads to one unchallenge-able conclusion on how public policy can maximise people's welfare. The optimum conditions prevail when government draws its revenue from the rents of land and natural resources. Why, then, do social scientists fail to prescribe this powerful tool for eradicating poverty? Let us assume that they are purely concerned with being practical. This leads to the advice that is stressed in a study produced by the World Bank's Infrastructure and Urban Development Department. The study was written by William Dillinger for the Bank and agencies of the United Nations. The author makes plain at the outset why his analysis would not commend the optimum pricing policy: "For all its economic virtues, the property tax carries a high political price".[1]

Repeatedly, the World Bank analyst restates—as if it were a mantra—that the property tax entails political costs. The policy was just too good—and too honest—to handle. So its capacity to deliver economic efficiency and democratic outcomes (such as transparency—no tax-by-stealth here) are held against it as a liability.

> From a political standpoint, the effectiveness of the property tax in confronting taxpayers with the costs of municipal services is no virtue. Central governments—which exercise veto power over property tax policy and frequently are responsible for its administration—are reluctant to allow the tax to be exploited effectively.[2]

So, the tool that would do most for the least effort to enable people to achieve their aspirations without hindrance from others (or their government) is skilfully side-lined. It is true that people do react with greater passion towards changes in their property tax than to other forms of exactions. This explains why UK governments, for example, have persistently avoided reforms that would make the property tax more effective. This timidity tells us that politicians are not willing to trust people with all the facts.

The property tax connects the payer directly with the benefits received from public services through their occupation (or other use) of land. This is the principle that we all apply and accept in the markets for consumer goods, without causing howls of protest: people expect to pay for what they receive. This contrasts with taxes that are concealed in the prices that consumers pay. When stealth tax rates are altered, protests are not vociferous. So politicians are tempted to avoid the property tax in favour of a hundred and one other ways to squeeze people's private incomes.

The outcome is under-use of the property tax (sacrificing efficiency) and resort to stealth taxes (sacrificing democratic ideals like transparency and personal responsibility). The material loss is enormous: Britain alone lost the equivalent of one year's output

Trading off the Truth

THE reforms which the IMF prescribes are wrapped up in language persuasively designed to convince the neo-colonised countries that its financial medicine is based on reason. For example, governments are repeatedly told that they face 'trade-offs' between high-return investment projects (as in infrastructure) and spending on health and education.

A classic example is the IMF's Public investment and fiscal policy—lessons from the Pilot Country Studies (2005).*

To avoid increasing their debt burden, the neo-colonised are informed that they face spending constraints and that hard choices have to be made between building a road and social welfare.

Backed by impressive research, the IMF brings the agenda round to its preferred approach. This "would entail an assessment of the scope for mobilising both private and public resources for infrastructure spending, within a macroeconomically sound and fiscally sustainable framework" (paragraph 16). This leads to the recommendation for funding public investment either by debt or the sale of state assets (paragraph 17, table 7). Decoded, this language is based on Orwellian doublethink.

- Taxes favoured by the IMF are unsustainable. They corrode enterprise from within by inflicting deadweight losses on the private sector—which consequently provokes the need for the state intervention that the IMF wishes to avoid.

- The sale of state assets—if these are land or natural resources—deprives the state of revenue in perpetuity from a source that would optimise the provision of public goods and so maximise the profitability of private enterprise.

Nowhere in the IMF's review does it commend the optimum strategy for maximising economic growth.

* www.imf.org/external/np/pp/eng/2005/040105a.pdf

of GDP during Tony Blair's 10-year premiership.[3] But the stakes are higher in the neo-colonised world, where people die every day because their leaders are intimidated by the doctrine of "a high political price" into employing inferior ways to raise revenue. There comes a time when the price of not doing what is right is too great. This is when people demand a strengthening of the moral and social fabric of their communities.

The philosophy of property rights and public finance, and the administration of these policies, are in a state of disarray. This is due more to ideological prejudice than lack of reason (an example is given in the box on the previous page). An informed public debate is needed before governments will muster the courage to embark on policies that deliver remedies. The starting point must be with that most revered of documents, the UN's Universal Declaration of Human Rights.

The UN *Universal Declaration of Human Rights*

Around the world, people campaign for human rights as never before. Curiously, however, the birthright to land receives rare acknowledgement. Collectively, we have forgotten the philosophy of sharing the resources of nature, a primordial right that was recognised by John Locke when he wrote Two Treatises on Government (1690). That is why it is one of the supreme ironies that Locke helped to lay the foundations of the modern power structure that excludes the majority from their right to land. The tradition which he helped to enshrine in law has disfigured the various bills of human rights in the 20th century, including the United Nations' attempt to pronounce on the right of people to be treated as equals.

In his account of the rules of governance (he called it a 'social contract'), Locke explained that everyone enjoyed the natural right to "life, liberty and estate".[4] That word estate is the old English legal concept for landed property. There was no ambiguity in Locke's exposition of natural rights: we all had the right to land, without which there could be no life. But he conceded that, in a commercial society, people could hold more land than they needed to meet their immediate needs, so long as they left enough land for others to use. But that provision—that everyone was entitled to access land—was not incorporated into his draft of the constitution for the settlers of Carolina. Instead, his provisions consolidated the monopoly of land for the English aristocrats who embarked on the most audacious land grab in history. Sanctioned by the power of the English state, the patricians of the Old World staked their claim to the lands of the New World and sealed the fate of the indigenous peoples.

Today, the property rights that were defined by Locke's successors are treated as sacred. Those rights, however, are wrapped up in documents that display a curious opaqueness, as if there was something to hide. The UN's Universal Declaration of Human Rights is the prime example. It affirms the right to private property in a way that (1) sanctions the deprivation of people's human rights, and (2) legitimises the appropriation of property that belongs to others.

The modern doctrine of human rights has abandoned its origins in natural rights. The doctrine has become little more than the expression of a vested interest. The constitutional documents of the US, for example, protect the version of property rights favoured by the heirs to the English aristocracy,[5] a historical reality that is obscured by the rhetorical claim that all citizens are treated as equals.

The United Nations adopted the Universal Declaration of Human Rights in 1948. This is the template against which we now judge the behaviour of individuals and of sovereign nations. It purports to define the rights of everyone on earth. Unfortunately, the exercise of those rights permits the institutionalised abuse of people in every country of the world.

- The Declaration fails to specify the preconditions for liberty. So even if we all complied with its strictures, people cannot secure their humanity because the individual's right to life is unenforceable.[6]
- The Declaration fails to specify the conditions for a healthy society. Obligations are placed on the state which cannot be fulfilled without abusing people's freedom, which includes their right to retain the property they create by their labour.

These defects render the Declaration inadequate to secure the universal rights as these were conceived under natural law.

Problems begin with the preamble, where the UN promotes "inalienable rights". Primordially, early humans acted as if they recognised the equal right of everyone to access nature's resources. This biologically-based 'right' gained formal recognition as humans acquired the cultural capacity to consciously express their inter-personal agreements. And yet, there is no reference to people's equal right of access to land or nature's resources in the UN document.

The UN records its disapproval of the barbarous acts which result from contempt for others. But those abuses were rarely inspired by the desire to deprive people of "employment", "housing" or "medical care"; in the significant cases of mass intrusion on the rights of others, the aggressors sought to appropriate the territory on which people were settled. And yet, the Declaration has no provision for restoring every person's equal right of access to, and use of, land.

Without land, the affirmation that people are "born free and equal in dignity and rights" (Article 1) is meaningless. In Article 2, we are assured that "everyone is entitled to all the rights and freedoms set forth in this Declaration". They are guaranteed freedom of religion, to get married and have children, to work and associate with others. But what they are not guaranteed is an entitlement to occupy the space they need on which to practice their religion, procreate, build their homes and work for their living.

Article 3 offers a variation on the Lockean theme. Whereas the philosopher wrote about the right to "life, liberty and estate", the UN in Article 3, offered "security of person" in place of estate (land). But without the guarantee of land, no-one's life can be secure.

The Declaration offers a crude portrait of the individual, who is treated as detached from nature and barely anchored in the community that gives personality its content. Thus its catalogue of rights are assigned to individuals in a sometimes empty rhetoric: who would one sue to secure a remedy for the right to employment?[7]

The Declaration grants society a grudging status. Where it is introduced, society is burdened with the responsibility to secure the rights of individuals without provision for it to acquire the necessary resources. In Article 28, for example, "Everyone is entitled to a social and international order in which the rights and freedoms set forth in this Declaration can be fully realised". But the Declaration falls short, and remains silent on the rights of a community against the individual. Where the individual is said to have a duty to the community (Article 29 [1]) the duties are not specified.

It is not possible for people in community to fulfil obligations without access to resources to fund the provision of public goods. Culture, for example, is acknowledged as indispensable for the dignity and development of personality (Article 22). Everyone "has the right to participate in the cultural life of the community, to enjoy the arts and to share in scientific advancement and its benefits" (Article 27 [1]). So we are entitled to the benefits of a civilisation. But civilisations are contingent on the ability of people to generate and share in the economic surplus (rents), without which there would be no culture, arts and science. And yet, the UN Declaration again is silent on the right of the community to claim those rents to fund culture. And it is silent on the duty of the individual to deliver those rents.

This places the nation-state in an invidious position. It is obliged (under Articles 21 and 22) to deliver public services to everyone, including social security, but the terms on which it may raise the funds to meet the costs are not specified. There is a right way and a wrong way to achieve this, and a person's liberties are infringed if the wrong choice is made.

- The wrong way is to tax the product of people's labour. This is an intrusion on private property that is possible only by exercising coercive power. Under the Declaration such revenue-raising instruments ought to be outlawed, unless there are extenuating circumstances in each case to justify the infringement of a person's liberty and private property.
- The right way is for the state to act as the guardian of the public value. In this case, the rents are freely yielded by the individual in exchange for the use of public goods. Under the Declaration, this financial expression of human rights and obligations

ought to be sanctioned as the pre-eminent method for raising revenue.

The omissions from the Declaration create an intolerable philosophical and legal situation, for the individual depends on a healthy society for the fulfilment of personal potential. The individual is recognised by the UN as a social being—someone with "honour and reputation" to protect (Article 12). But this means that, for the individual to equip the community with the means that lead to the enforcement of personal rights, revisions to the Declaration are imperative.

The need to fill the void in the UN Declaration is urgent, for sovereign states today are unable to meet their responsibilities. In Britain, for example, more than 25% of households are deemed to be 'breadline poor'.[8] Those households are dependent on the state for subsistence, a dependency that undermines their right to the dignity that comes with the ability to pay one's way through life. Britain, despite its tax exactions, is not able to fulfil its obligation to enable everyone to live the life visualised by the UN Declaration.

If an honest politician were to propose that all of the rental income of a person's land should be paid to offset the cost of the services that give his site its utility, the howl would go up: confiscation. Legal action would probably follow on the grounds that government was taking the property of its owner. We need to untangle the mess behind property rights.

- Criminals who reallocate the possession of articles that we have earned the right to possess by our labours are left in no doubt about what law-abiding citizens think of them. They are imprisoned.
- When people walk away with publicly-created wealth,

however, action is not taken to restore that property to the rightful owners. The owners are the people who, by their presence and co-operative activities in the community, originate that value. Yet, their deprivation is sanctioned by law.

Why don't we think it is appropriate to throw into gaol the people who steal the public value? Because the UN ritualises a doctrine of property that makes respectable the private appropriation of that value. To alter this state of affairs, we need a new understanding about the way governments fund public services. For a start, the language that biases the way governments frame their revenue policies needs to be clarified. An example is the emphatic statement by the World Bank that "in principle there is no 'right' rate of property tax".[9] This tells us more about the mind-set of the authors than about economic theory, morality or the process of producing and exchanging wealth. There is a right rate: 100%—the full price—of the stream of urban and agricultural rents, nature's minerals, and the absorption capacity of the environment. These rents equal the benefits of services delivered to users. They are the measure of what people are willing—and actually do—pay. So the only question is who collects the rents. The agencies that provide the services, or strangers?

Intellectuals in the neo-colonised world—be they in politics, academia, the media or civil society's NGOs—have the resources to engage in an enquiry into the rules of governance to determine what would best serve the needs of their communities. They have the intellectual capacity to set aside the prejudices inherited from the colonial past. They should be on their guard against the constitutional jargon that does not protect people's primary rights. Fiscal practice and legal preaching need to be harmonised, if the riches of territories are to be shared by all. Fine words, even the right words, are not enough, as we learn from the case of Ethiopia.

Beyond Athenian Democracy:
Ethiopia & the Fiscal Imperative

Conflicts over natural resources arise because societies fail to neutralise those riches as the source of contention. For so long as they are available to some, they will be fought over by others.

Traditionally, governments were controlled by people with property. This applies to the democracies, as well as governance by aristocratic elites or tyrants. It was only in the 20th century that the property qualification (mainly the ownership of land) was separated from the right to vote.

The provision that the ownership of property qualified one to vote was built into the politics of the 'land of the free'. Joseph Galloway, one of the Founding Fathers of the USA, (quoted by Merrill Jensen) put it in these terms:

> 'Power results from the real property of society,' he said. 'The states of Greece, Macedon, Rome were founded on this plan,' and the English is founded on the same principle, the principle of the representation of landed property in the government of the state.[10]

Ethiopia is the one nation in Africa that was not colonised by a European power. Its roots can be traced back to the first kingdom, founded about the 11th century BC. The Homeric poems celebrate a pious people who were often visited by the gods. We pick up their history in 1974. The Derg regime, composed of members of the army, had deposed Emperor Haile Selassie and proclaimed 'Ethiopian Socialism'. All land was nationalised and strict price controls were introduced for agricultural and industrial products. The collectivisation of farming proved disastrous, and the Derg was deposed in 1991.

Thereafter followed a process of consultation among the country's 60m people on the rights to land which they wanted embedded in a new constitution. They participated at the kebelle (village) level, and over 90% of weredas (districts) completed and returned questionnaire forms showing how people had voted. The constitution of the Federal Democratic Republic of Ethiopia was ratified by the Constitutional Assembly on December 8, 1994.

On land ownership, overwhelming support was expressed for the view that land should be treated as a social asset. This was formalised in Article 40 (paragraph 3) of the Constitution, which states:

> The right of ownership of rural and urban land, as well as of all natural resources, is exclusively vested in the State and in the peoples of Ethiopia. Land is a common property of the nations, nationalities and peoples of Ethiopia and shall not be subject to sale or to other means of transfer.

Researcher Gail Warden reviewed the constitutional provisions on land tenure. She concluded that Ethiopia should resist pressure from the West, which wanted the country to legalise the sale of land as a commodity. Pointing out that much property in New York City is leasehold, which did not impede economic development, she observed: "Ethiopia is being encouraged to do what the West says, and not what it actually does".[11]

Land really was available to anyone who needed it in Ethiopia. Furthermore, because it was illegal to sell land, peasants who might have been tempted to cash in their assets and migrate to the cities were inhibited from doing so. But for those who did choose to go in search of urban employment and lifestyles, the leasehold system ensured that residential plots would be made available at affordable rents.

But the formal provisions in the Constitution were not flawless. For while peasants could not sell their tracts, they could lease them to neighbours for payment in kind. The implication is crucial. While all the land is in the public domain, some of its rental income (whether in cash or kind) could be privatised. And, ultimately, what land grabbers want is not the physical land or resource, but the rental income.

The Ethiopian Constitution was reviewed by the late Sir Kenneth Jupp, who had served as a judge in the English High Court for 15 years. Sir Kenneth admired the provisions in the Constitution that based the allocation of land on the leasehold system, but he feared that insufficient attention had been paid to ensuring that rents remained in the public domain. Despite the guarantee that land would be made available to those who needed it, Sir Kenneth understood that there was a finite supply in the locations where people chose to live and work. These sites were the most valuable, and it was not possible to allocate equal strips of such land to everyone in Ethiopia (let alone to secure the rights of future generations). Therefore, it was vital that the equalisation of land rights should find its reciprocal in the fiscal system. Regular revaluation of rents, at market prices, would enable government to collect the revenue to fund services that everyone shared. Otherwise, the following was possible:

> If the farmers and pastoralists get their land free, then those with a surplus will soon become a class superior to the unfortunates who use land near or at the margin. In time, some will be able to lease out some or all

of their land and draw rent from letting others work it. This superiority then becomes the basis for ethnic discontent and regional conflict as the losers perceive that others, on more fertile or advantageously located land, are accumulating material resources faster than they are, for reasons unrelated to their skill, enterprise, or endeavour.[12]

The people who drafted Ethiopia's Constitution understood the economics of the land market, and they were determined to remove land as the site of social contest. But the wisdom that informed the law on land also needed to be embedded in public finance.

To complete the democratic revolution in Ethiopia, therefore, provision needs to be made to regularly reappraise the public value of land. The information needs to be stored in records that are accessible at a low cost to everyone. This would facilitate not just the collection of the public value. It is the first step towards developing a public consciousness in favour of safeguarding rents as public revenue. It would, for example, combat corruption: if people know the size of the public value, they would intervene if some of it disappeared into Swiss bank accounts.

The educational function of a sound constitution is crucial to secure an informed electorate. The UN advocates that school children should be instructed on its Universal Declaration of Human Rights. But given that birthrights to land do not feature in the syllabus of schools, the UN assists the rent-privatisers in their agenda—cultivating a selective amnesia so that people are inhibited from thinking about their most fundamental of natural rights.

8

Settlers & the Land Tax

Settler Model I:
Hong Kong & Public Finance

Lord palmerston was scathing about the territory Britain
acquired as a toehold on China: "a barren rock with nary
a house upon it—it will never be a mart for trade". That
was in 1841, after Palmerston had successfully waged the Opium
War that secured Britain's right to sell narcotics to the Emperor's
subjects. Today, Hong Kong is the freest, richest, most dynamic of
entrepreneurial economies in the world. It is rated as No. 1 in the
Index of Economic Freedom compiled by The Wall Street Journal
and the Washington DC-based Heritage Foundation, a free market
think tank.[1] All of this, and the land is not freehold, and never
was.

But this key to Hong Kong's success is treated by Western
diplomatic, economic and political commentators as if it were a
shameful state secret. And it is true that Hong Kong's success does

offend capitalism's most cherished belief, that land must be held as freehold if resources are to be efficiently allocated.

In 1843, Britain hoisted the Union flag and proclaimed that all land would remain with the Crown. Freehold would not feature in this colony. Instead, leases would be granted for 75 years, the period considered necessary to induce tenants to construct buildings. Other sites would be allocated on 21-year leases.[2]

Leasehold was not employed for the reason that it was the correct economic policy, however. Britain had acquired the rock from the Emperor on a lease that terminated on June 30, 1997. Therefore, it did not make legal sense to offer land as freehold, when such a right could not be enforced beyond the terms of the Crown's lease with China.

So Britain, the emerging epicentre of the global capitalist order, became landlord for anyone who wished to trade in the oriental markets. Leases were sold at public auctions or granted directly by the Crown, as landlord, in return for an annual rent. Subsequently, leasehold periods were altered, as were the terms for paying rent to the exchequer. But the principle was preserved: if you wanted to make money in Hong Kong, you had to pay rent to the British government which used the revenue to fund the infrastructure.[3] As a result of this financial formula, entrepreneurs were able to trade without carrying a heavy tax burden. This gave the value-adding producers a competitive edge in the global markets.

This was as close to a laboratory experiment as one could get to test the theory advanced by Adam Smith, that the rent of land was the "peculiarly suitable" source of revenue for a commercial society. The development of the economy proved so successful that, in 2006, it produced a GDP (measured in purchasing power parity: PPP) of $30,822, compared with the UK's $30,821. Unlike the UK, however, Hong Kong could not draw on reserves of coal and oil to fuel her prosperity. Primary materials and food had to be imported. Even so, Hong Kong enjoyed one advantage over her colonial master: people-power, unburdened by the income tax.

Just before the colony was returned to Mao's successors in 1997, the Hong Kong government was providing 3m people with subsidised housing. The mass transit system was the envy of mayors who presided over cities in the West, its funding coming out of the value added to the land rents by the transport system itself.[4] Here was a classic case of the self-funding formula that fostered personal liberty in the open economy.

- Why, when politicians preach to governments of the neo-colonised world, do they fail to expound the lessons of Hong Kong?
- Why, when financial agencies offer development loans, do they attach strings that deliver the opposite results to those achieved by the tax-and-tenure policies of Hong Kong?

Hong Kong proves that institutions—combined with the enterprise of free people—are the keys to prosperity. Territory does not have to be richly endowed with natural resources. The key is the combination of property rights and public finance. Once the rents that people produce together are ring-fenced as the revenue to be spent on the common good, the scope for corruption and bad governance is severely diminished, and the productive talents of people are liberated.

Hong Kong's tax-and-tenure formula lays the foundation for the economics of material abundance.

Settler Model II:
Argentina & Land Grabbing

In the history of colonialism, attempts were made to adopt policies similar to Hong Kong's. Their failures offer lessons to countries that wish to become prosperous. Argentina's history is illuminating. A sophisticated attempt was made to prevent land being grabbed to the detriment of future generations.

In 1824, Bernardino Rivadavia introduced a land law for the province of Buenos Aires. The law was extended to the rest of the country in 1826 when Rivadavia became Argentina's first president. The extensive lands—the pampas, the size of France—would be allocated to users who would pay rent to the community. The nation would retain dominion over the territory and would fund the public's services out of the rents that people were willing to pay to use the rich soils to grow wheat or as pasture for cattle.

The logic of this policy was explained to the British government by Dr. Ignacio Núñez, Rivadavia's diplomatic envoy, who said that "the spirit of the project is that publicly-owned land should never be held in any way other than by leaseholds...The present taxes bear harmfully upon the people and hinder [the country's] development...The rent of land is the most solid and definite source of revenue on which the State must count". Núñez argued that the collection of land rent would make it possible to abolish tariffs and all other taxes.[5]

Rent was payable at a yearly rate of 8% on the value of pasture lands and 4% on cultivated lands. Leases were on 20-year terms, with revision of rents at the end of 10 years after reassessments by local juries. This would ensure that, as the economy grew, the rental surplus would be recycled back into the public purse for investment in the additional infrastructure that an expanding population needs.

It was an inspirational programme with the potential to lay the foundations of prosperity for future waves of settlers into this vast territory. The condition for securing this outcome was the willingness to enforce the terms of the land law. Unfortunately, the people who acquired estates found ways to avoid their obligations. This became possible as regional governors (caudillos, or bosses) resisted Rivadavia's approach to governance. Rivadavia was relying on a strong central government through which to implement progressive policies for the whole territory. The caudillos favoured a federal political structure, which would place the administration of property rights in their hands; giving them the power to undermine the land law. With the fall of Rivadavia, estate owners acquired the influence to evade their fiscal obligations: they manipulated their communities to secure the undervaluation of land. This deprived the public purse of revenue, and ranchers evolved a lifestyle based on the consumption of rents with the least effort possible directed towards the efficient use of their holdings.

Critics have blamed the land law, arguing that Rivadavia neglected to take account of the rapacity of human nature or heed that temporary concessions could be converted into permanent arrangements. These are not legitimate criticisms. As we have seen in the case of Hong Kong, which we may assume had its share of rapacious individuals, leaseholds were enforced to the financial benefit of both the government and the people who traded in the colony.

Argentina turned out to be another case in which sound institutions were sacrificed because the majority failed to defend their legal and moral rights. The predators were allowed to manipulate the law in a manner that would redirect social evolution along a false path that was not sustainable. In 1914, thanks to the export of beef and wheat to Europe, Argentina was the fifth or sixth wealthiest nation in the world. A century later, in 2006, she was receiving aid from donor countries that once purchased her food.

An attempt was made to revive the rent-as-public-revenue policy in the 1970s when a lawyer, Fernando Scornik Gerstein, was appointed advisor on land taxation to the ministers of economics and agriculture. In 1975, he chaired the Special Commission on Land Taxation established by the Ministry of Agriculture. But then, anticipating the military coup of 1976, Gerstein departed for Spain, and "with the rightist military takeover, all ideas of tax reform were abandoned, and the Special Committee was dissolved".[6]

Argentina failed to seal her cultural foundations with the rents that could be produced by the people, so history shifted on to the path that was typical of the fate of Latin colonies. Once one of the abundant food larders of the world, in 1997 Argentina was shamed by the need to import cheaper Australian beef to keep near-bankrupt processing enterprises operating.

To derive insights from the past, economic historians compare Argentina and Australia because of their similarities. Tax-and-tenure policies proved to be the major difference, accounting for the striking dissimilarities in the prosperity of these two countries in the 20th century (see table below).

Argentina and Australia Change of Fortune: Selected Vital Statistics (2006)		
	Argentina	Australia
Population (million)	38.4	20.1
Territory (million km²)	2.7	7.6
Unemployment (%)	13.6	5.5
GDP (PPP) per capita ($)	13,298	30,331

Argentina and Australia Change of Fortune: Selected Vital Statistics (2006)		
Tax revenue (% of GDP)	14.2	24.1
Official development assistance ($m)—multilateral	27	none
Official development assistance ($m)—bilateral	94	none

Source: Kane, Holmes and O'Grady (2007)

Settler Model III: Australia & Public Rent Revenue

In 1890, in per capita terms Australia was the richest nation on earth. She eclipsed income in the United States by a remarkable 41% (see table over). The frenetic land speculation that preceded the depression of 1890 was the turning point in her No. 1 status. The severity of the crash is explained by "the magnitude and speculative nature of the preceding boom and the impact of a severe drought".[7] Drought was an act of nature, from which the settlers were able to recover. The real 'blight' which plagued the Australian continent throughout the 20th century was the propensity to abuse —and to speculate in—the rents of land.

The Sachs thesis—that the abundance of nature's resources is a constraint on growth—was certainly false in the Australian case. Here, favourable institutional arrangements in the 19th century "ensured that resource abundance became a blessing rather than a curse". Ian McLean, an economic historian at the University of Adelaide, asked in one of his studies: Why Was Australia so Rich?

Levels of per capita GDP 1820-1994 (relative to the US) (US = 100)			
	Australia	UK	Argentina
1820	119	136	n/a
1850	169	130	n/a
1870	155	133	53
1890	141	121	63
1900	105	113	67
1913	104	95	72
1929	74	76	63
1938	92	98	66
1950	75	72	52
1973	75	72	48
1994	76	73	37

Source: Maddison (1995) Appendix D

Australia was born rich, attaining an income per capita higher than any other country after little more than half a century of European settlement. Further, for nearly two centuries Australia has remained (relatively) rich, despite some short-term slippages....Contrary to the view of many growth economists that it is a curse to be resource rich, natural resource abundance must figure prominently in any persuasive answer to the question posed in the title of this paper.[8]

A young, male settler population—partly due to the British policy of exporting convicts—made it possible to achieve high levels of productivity in the production of wool and gold. But there was more to the story than the resource endowment and the demographic profile. The institutional arrangements in the mining industry "helped ensure that the resources contributed to broader economic growth rather than rents accruing to just a limited segment of the population".[9]

But international comparisons of per capita GDP disguise the real story about living standards at the end of the 19th century. For Australians chose to reduce the hours they worked to improve the quality of their lives. Once this benefit was factored in, the "leisure-augmented income" rises from 9% to 18% above that achieved in the UK in 1913.[10] This was one benefit of ready access to land, which—in the second half of the 19th century—made it possible for labour to raise productivity and claim its rewards in cash and the quality-of-life free people chose for themselves.[11]

It was different at the beginning when settlement began with the scramble to grab as much land as possible. In due course, however, the British Crown secured the sub-division of land into family farms through land acts in the 1860s and 1870s. This resulted in a wide distribution of ownership.

The contrast between Argentina and Australia is especially telling here, given the likely importance of these differing initial institutional arrangements to the later divergence in growth rates between these two economies.[12]

This is not a sufficient assessment. Although large holdings were allocated in Argentina, this was in conjunction with rental charges set at market levels. If those rents had been collected, and consistently reassessed as the economy grew, the owners would have had to put their holdings to best use. They would have had to achieve the same levels of productivity as was achieved by farmers on smaller holdings. This would have pressured the estate owners to employ many more people, thereby competing for labour and raising wages. If the owners failed to adopt these practices, they could not have met their rental obligations. That would have obliged them to relinquish some of their acres to others. So the fiscal policy, correctly administered, would have achieved results similar to those in Australia. It was to avoid this prospect that provincial governors resisted Rivadavia's policies. This left estate owners free to underuse their land without financial penalty. The costs were transferred to the pool of dependent workers, while increasing the political power of estate owners over the landless.

The leasehold system was put to better use in Australia. In 1847, New South Wales introduced regulations that based tenure on fixed-term leases. One consequence was "a more egalitarian distribution of land ownership, limiting in turn the political power of the pastoralists. The contrasting history of land disposal policies in Argentina, and of the political influence of large landowners there, is a salutary reminder of what might have been".[13]

One reason why Australia adopted public charges on rents was to break up large holdings. A second reason was that the settlers wanted to fund infrastructure to support the agricultural and mining industries.[14] In 1879, Queensland was the first colony to abandon the English property tax (imposed on both land and the improvements on it—ie the buildings, etc), to levy municipal charges on the capital value of land excluding improvements.[15]

Economists who emphasise institutions to explain economic growth stress the role played by the retention of European practices. In Australia, however, the settlers came to realise that the English property tax discouraged investment in improvements on the land. That was why "they quickly discarded it for a rate based not on total property income but on the market or selling price of raw land which became known as the system of rating on the 'Unimproved Capital Value'".[16] State governments switched to the land value based charge beginning with Victoria (in 1877), Tasmania (1880), South Australia (1884), New South Wales (1895) and Queensland (1915). The new Federal Government enacted the Land Tax Act in 1911, which remained in place until it was abolished in 1952.

At the outbreak of World War I, Australian governments were raising a significant part of public revenue from rents. But with each passing decade—even as increasing prosperity brought a rising total rent—the fiscal philosophy was debased, with a lengthening catalogue of exemptions that reduced the share of rents collected to fund public goods. A seminal study by Terry Dwyer (see graph over) reported that total land and resource rents, publicly collected and not, were 8.85% of GDP in 1911. A century later, in 2005, they were 32%, but little of it was now collected fairly and directly for the public purse. (Although much of the rent was captured indirectly through the use of distortionary taxes.) Douglas Herps, a senior valuer and consultant to the Commonwealth Grants Commission, estimated that "the magnitude of Australia's economic rent is such that it could provide at least 50% of all the country's present inflated taxation".[17]

Despite the policy retreats during the 20th century, however, Australia managed to cling on to the concept of rent as public revenue. This helped to secure the modern-isation of the economy. Her territory was three times that of Argentina in size, but Argentina had the advantage of people-power: these people could have raised urban rents to levels at least equal to those in Australia. If those rents had been used to fund shared services, the GDP of Argentina could have matched Australia's (see tables on p. 143 & p. 144). But a similar remonstration can be levelled against Australia. Her GDP per capita was $30,331 in 2006. It could have been significantly higher (and greater than that achieved by the US) but for the cyclical booms and busts in the property market which repeatedly disrupted growth.[18]

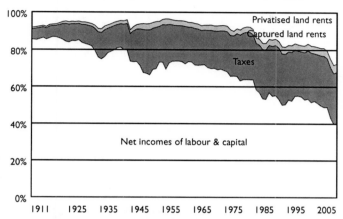

Classical Components of GDP – Australia 1911-2005

Source: Dwyer (2003), Kavanagh (2007)

We can only imagine how much more prosperous and en-vironmentally secure Australia would be today if she had re-mained constant in the application of the rent-as-public-revenue policy. According to Bryan Kavanagh, adjusting for the lost investments and disruptions caused by real estate specula-tion just for the years since 1972, GDP in 2006 could have been AU$1 trillion higher than was actually achieved. Even with conservative estimates, the GDP lost due to the use of taxes that damaged the economy resulted in the deprivation of AU$35,000 per year for every man, woman and child.[19]

Implementing the tax reform agenda in the 21st century requires pioneers with the courage and imagination to lead the way from poverty to prosperity. We shall conclude this study by explaining why three countries of the redeveloping world could pioneer poli-cies that would kick-start their societies on a path of growth that secured fair shares for everyone, immediately transforming the prospects for peace and prosperity around the globe.

9

Social Capitalism

Pioneer for Prosperity: South Africa?

Studies by the IMF and the World Bank report that tax rates are the main constraint on the private sector.[1] Economic bottlenecks attributable to inadequate provision of infrastructure (such as transport) are also identified as a major obstacle to economic growth. But the IMF, in analysing the relationship between public investment and tax policy, secures the answers it wants to highlight its preference for the private provision of public goods—with the taxpayer incurring the major risks of investment in capital-intensive infrastructure.

We have shown that public finance policies and the provision of infrastructure can be united in a self-funding arrangement that works with the grain of both human dignity and market economics. Why, then, do the IMF and the World Bank play fast and loose with the policy of property taxation? One answer is to be found in the fact that the IMF's research favours private and foreign sources of revenue and Western property rights. Studiously, the IMF remains uninformative on the potential for raising funds from domestic sources on the back of improvements in infrastructure.

We can assume that the fiscal reform we propose would, at first sight, worry property owners. But that is why democratic debate, to achieve popular understanding, is vital. People who wish to take charge of their lives—and the destinies of their communities— need to arrive at a consensus for change based on access to knowledge that the IMF is not in a hurry to deliver.

- Only by introducing a fully functional pricing mechanism for the public sector does it become possible to neutralise the monopoly power that is otherwise handed to the private owners of nature's resources.
- Only by restructuring the distribution of income in favour of those who work and invest in the creation of capital goods, does it become possible to achieve the UN's Millennium Development Goals.

This is the model for social capitalism. There is no back-street route to this outcome. If these two insights are not enshrined in laws and economic processes, there is no prospect of achieving sustainable growth and the evolution of balanced communities. For a society that operates outside this framework is necessarily exploitative, depleting both human potential and the riches of nature—and ingraining poverty into the fabric of society.

The concept of social capitalism would be dismissed by most socialists as a contradiction in terms. But if further empirical evidence is needed, where better to find it than South Africa? The African National Congress was democratically elected. Its ideology was rooted in socialism, but—once in power—it pragmatically turned to the free market. It could have embarked on a radical fiscal reform, for South Africa had in place an effective administration of site-value taxation. This locally-administered charge was employed in municipal jurisdictions that held approximately 70% of the nation's land value, and was an effective rent-collecting fiscal tool.[2]

Politically, the ANC and Nelson Mandela achieved a monumental feat. They mobilised blacks and whites behind a common agenda of social renewal. Their constitution contained fine words about the rights of the individual. But (as we saw in chapter 6), the doctrine of ownership rights in the nation's natural resources needs practical expression on the ground (literally on the ground) (see box).

The post-apartheid republic could have elevated its municipal site-value tax to a national fiscal strategy. This would have delivered justice between the races, and it would have placed the economy on a new—accelerated—growth path that included the people of the shanty towns. Instead, in 2004, with its Property

---

Terror (I)

THE roadside piles of stone missiles near slums were a familiar sight in apartheid South Africa. They were revived in the rural township of Boikhutso, where residents of the tin-shack dwellings rioted and stoned cars in frustration at the lack of economic progress.* They had hoped, post-apartheid, to dispense with bucket toilets and the other symbols of deprivation. The Rev. Moses Moshelane, the local municipal manager, said: "The expectations of people are too high and too fast. And while you are busy addressing one squatter area, another one mushrooms somewhere else."

* *Financial Times*, June 5, 2007

Rating Act, the government scrapped the land-only tax in favour of a tax that also fell on capital investments on the land. This was the version of the property tax favoured by the IMF. The new law consequently introduced a penalty on people who invested their

Social Capitalism

money and enterprise on land. In the case of Cape Town, the amendment bequeathed the owners of idle land an annual gift of approximately 136 million rand.[3]

The bias against people who worked and invested was a fundamental policy error. We may assume that the consequences were not intended by a government that genuinely wished to help low-income citizens. Fortunately, however, because of its administrative history, it would be easy for South Africa to revert back to a site-value-only charge.

The price of not doing so would be crippling. Without the property rights and public finance that favour the common good, South Africa is not entitled to claim that it champions justice and efficiency. And since the synthesis of these two is the precondition for consigning poverty to history in that country, nor may it claim to speak for the poor.

In the case of South Africa, the outcomes specified in chapter 8 would be achieved at the end of a relatively short transition. South Africa could pioneer the advance to economic equality in Africa. The alternative outcome has been foreseen by Desmond Tutu, the former Archbishop of Cape Town, who warned that the gap between rich and poor was widening. "We are sitting on a powder keg over the matter of redistribution of wealth," observed Tutu, one of the charismatic leaders of the anti-apartheid movement. Most of the people living in shacks before the end of white rule were still living in shacks. The poor had remained patient, and Tutu found it hard "to explain why they don't say to hell with Tutu, Mandela and the rest, and go on the rampage".[4] Politicians were aware that a crisis was looming. The alternative was ominously identified by a spokesman (Eddie Mohoebi) for the South African government's Agriculture and Land Affairs Ministry:

It is clear that, short of nationalisation of land, there is a need for drastic measures to be implemented, to intervene in the land market to accelerate redistribution.[5]

The only way to synthesise all competing interests—to unite commercial imperatives with ancient attitudes towards the land as culturally and spiritually central to the lives of the people living on it—is through fiscal reform.

Pioneer for Prosperity: India?

Seven years after Jeffrey Sachs promoted an 8% growth target, India celebrated the 60th anniversary of her independence. It was a time for national celebration, but still Prime Minister Dr. Manmohan Singh had to lament malnutrition rates as a "national shame". Gandhi's dream of a free India, he decla-red, "will only be fully realised when we banish poverty from our midst". Almost half of India's children are underfed, with about 160,000 dying every year before reaching their first birthday.[6]

India, as one of the high-growth countries, was not immune from the widening of the gap between the rich and the poor. It had fallen victim of the capitalist growth disease. The number of her people living below $1-a-day is almost equal to the number in sub-Sahara Africa—300m.[7]

Economic inequality in Asia is approaching levels in Latin America. According to a professor of economics at the University of California (Berkeley), if current trends continue, China may soon reach the high-inequality levels of Brazil, Mexico and Chile.[8]

Inequality in India, measured in terms of land distribution, is greater than in China.[9] This is one of the outcomes of the land

Social Capitalism

boom in India which has enriched the few—such as KP Singh, the country's real estate baron whose fortune is estimated at £16.3bn.

Land is increasingly an explosive issue in India, where incomplete reforms have left much of the country in the hands of a few. This has led to riots and armed insurrection against attempts to industrialise large parts of India's interior.[10]

In October 2007, a landless army of 25,000 marched on Delhi.[11] This was the legacy of socialism's failure to provide the antidote to capitalism's growth disease. And yet, India preserves a collective memory of the value of shared rights in the community's land. India is, therefore, equipped to modernise the commons model of property rights so that the traditional benefits that flowed from social solidarity may be absorbed into the commercial economy.

As an example of a transitional mechanism towards the general solution that we discussed in chapter 8, India could designate swathes of her slums as Community Land Trusts (CLTS) (see box facing). This would be an alternative to the decision taken in 2007 by the government in New Delhi to demolish the tin shacks and construct dwellings for displaced families. The slum-dwellers were hostile to the plans, because the government also announced its intention to auction the land to the highest bidders. The poor had good reason to be anxious. Conventional urban renewal is based on property rights inherited from colonial times, when investment in real estate entailed the displacement of low income people. And yet, alternative possibilities exist even under the current tax-and-tenure regime.

In Mumbai, for example, Dharavi is the largest slum in Asia, occupying publicly-owned land. Here, the land problem could be neutralised by adopting the CLT model—removing land as a class—and in India, a caste—weapon. All of the future growth of rental income would be pooled back into the community and devoted to health clinics, educational amenities or whatever people needed. The CLT arrangement would enable residents (through, for example, management organisations) to shape the spending programmes funded out of the ground-rents that they paid into their community's purse.

The employment prospects would be significant, not least in construction. Using modern methods, structures could be built at less cost than conventional building techniques. And local labour could be trained to use the innovative methods that have been tested in countries such as Malaysia and China. Families would pay an annual rent for the land they occupied. The private home and

---

Community Land Trusts

LAND-SHARING is not anathema even in capitalist countries. In the USA, for example, the first Community Land Trust was established in 1968. There are now 186 CLTs across forty states and in Washington DC.*

The stock of homes is evenly split between owned and rented units. Buyers pay for the building, and the CLT retains ownership of the land. When the house is sold, the CLT usually has the right to repurchase it at a price that takes into account the value of improvements to the property and changes in local house prices.

Originally, CLTs were established by private groups. But this mechanism for providing affordable homes to low-income families has attracted local governments and public sector financing.

A similar movement is growing in Scotland, where the new parliament has made community land-sharing the centrepiece of its programme of land reform.

* Greenstein and Sungu-Eryilmaz (2007)

---

the shared rights to land would bind the inhabitants into holistic communities that fulfilled traditional cultural norms while working with the dynamics of the modern economy. By pioneering this approach in Asia, India would demonstrate that the urban crises that are intensifying everywhere in the world can be addressed locally in a socially inclusive way.

Extending the CLT model into the villages would begin the process of rebalancing the relationship between town and country. The millions who are liable to quit their small-holdings for tin shacks in towns would acquire incentives to remain in the countryside, as they enforced their rights to common land.[12]

Stemming the rural exodus is vital if India is to develop sustainable rates of growth. At present, investment in infrastructure such as roads deepens the income divide, and consequently encourages migration down the nation's improved highways (see box facing). By reforming public finance, rents would be available to upgrade rural infrastructure and automatically increase the living standards of those on the lowest incomes. This, in turn, would ease the pressure on urban infrastructure and enable people to diversify into new forms of economic activity. By diffusing higher living standards, India could pioneer the retrieval of authentic local culture while engaging with the world of global commerce.

Pioneer for Prosperity: Venezuela?

Democracy is canvassed as the practical and ethical model for resolving competing claims. As such, it is advanced as the reason for many international initiatives. We need to explore the proposition, because for many people in the neo-colonised world this doctrine is a smokescreen to advance the vital interests

Equity in Highways

RURAL infrastructure is crucial to development, yet "little is known about the size and especially the distribution of benefits from such investments in less developed countries", according to World Bank economist Hanan Jacoby. This is curious, for German agricultural economist Johann von Thünen (1783-1850) explained the economics of highway infrastructure long ago. Essentially, the better the road network, the lower the transport costs and the higher the land rent.

Jacoby tested this theory with land value data collected by the Nepal Living Standards Survey (1995-96).* By building a new road, would rents rise? He confirmed von Thünen's theory, but his approach is more interesting for what it reveals about the mindset of post-classical economists.

Jacoby's conclusions were coloured by his assumption that a new road would be funded by foreign aid. Why not assume that the road is funded out of the value which it adds as a result of improving productivity? Clawing back the increased rents would deliver startlingly different outcomes to those perceived by Jacoby.

- Politically, the state would not be in debt to foreign lenders.

- Economically, there would be little justification for Jacoby's claim that "rural road construction is certainly not the magic bullet for poverty alleviation".

- Socially, the bias in the distribution of benefits to owners with the most valuable land would be eliminated. For if the rents were collected, these net gains would be shared by everyone through their equal enjoyment of rent-funded public amenities.

As Jacoby notes, landless households do not benefit at all from road construction because the increase in wages is offset by price rises (like the cost of renting one's home). But there is no law of nature which says that this is an unavoidable outcome.

* Jacoby (2000)

of the West.

We have seen that the fundamental cause of poverty is the way that property rights and tax policies interact. The tensions within this process define capitalism. So tampering with that matrix is a threat to the system itself; and is—naturally—likely to provoke a hostile reaction. Is democracy per se the answer? Or is the vigour with which

---

Terror (2)

"THOSE familiar with recent Indian history will recognise one rather stark difference in the political ethos. The areas most associated with Maoist insurgency movements [are] all landlord areas. Looking at crime statistics also points to the landlord areas being most conflict-ridden....[L]andlord areas have higher levels of crime than non-landlord areas. Further, the difference is mainly in the levels of violent crime (which includes dacoities [armed robberies])."*

* Banerjee and Iyer (2005) p. 25

---

the West advocates the adoption of democratic institutions a covert way of preserving those elements of capitalism that injure people's vital interests? To understand what underlies the political failures of Western nations on the global stage, we shall consider the traumatic relationship between the US and Venezuela following the election of Hugo Rafael Chávez Frías.

The majority in Venezuela did declare their preferences in democratic terms. They turned to one of their own kind for help. Poverty had increased over the two decades prior to the election of Chávez, but their material deprivation was not because of the niggardliness of nature: over the past 25 years the country received $600bn in oil revenues. So, was democracy sufficient to deliver prosperity? If anyone in Venezuela was sceptical, cynicism seemed warranted by attempts to subvert the democratic will.

Chávez, the champion of peasants, achieved power with a majority of 60% of the popular vote. His presidential agenda was clear to everybody from the start: help the poor. His 'mistake' was to promote land reform. The reaction of the US to the Enabling Act (2001) was immediate. Its ambassador in Caracas, Donna Hrinak, declared: "The Land Law is an attack on the right of private property".[13] Chávez exacerbated relations with America by linking his agenda to socialism. This was a red rag to a bull in Washington DC.

Here was a president who felt confident that he could effect substantial improvement in the welfare of people who lived on less than $2-a-day in a nation that enjoyed a fabulous flow of oil-rents. Did it make any difference that he was proposing to promulgate his reforms on the back of a democratic mandate? Chávez was leading what he called a Bolivarian Revolution, delivering his "socialism of the 21st century".

His policies for land reform, because they were divorced from fiscal reform, would not work. Furthermore, they made enemies of the landed elites who took for granted their right to govern the nation. So a degree of tension within Venezuela was inevitable, but wasn't the democratic process supposed to facilitate peaceful resolutions to potential conflicts of interest?

In the past, because of the colonial origins of the dist-ribution of land and power, peasant leaders vented their frustrations on their near neighbour, the USA. But a new maturity is needed if Latin America is finally to escape colo-nial bondage. As Lula, Brazil's President—a trade unionist who also achieved power by democratic means—stressed:

A long time ago I learned not to put the blame for backwardness in Brazil on the US. We have to blame ourselves. Our backwardness is caused by an elite which for a century didn't think about the majority and subordinated itself to foreign interests.[14]

But Chávez discovered that the mantle of democracy was no protection from his neighbour to the north. There was little love lost between the two governments once Chávez made it clear that he was going to redistribute land. Democratic mandate or not, the US government wanted Chávez removed. Millions of US tax dollars were channelled into Caracas to engineer regime change.

- The US, through its embassy and non-governmental agencies that had received funds from American taxpayers, sponsored a coup in 2002. It failed. Venezuelans took to the streets to demand the return of their president to the seat of government.
- Next, the US sponsored economic sabotage in the form of a 64-day 'national strike'. This was an employer-led lock-out. The oil taps on which the government relied for its revenue were illegally turned off by a private enterprise that was partly funded by the US government. That, too, failed.
- Having survived these anti-democratic actions, Chávez became the target of a massive disinformation operation. The costs incurred in disseminating the black arts of propaganda were borne by US taxpayers. That campaign against the democratically-elected president continues.

The documentary evidence for the claim that the US inspired and funded these hostile attacks on a democratically elected head of state was obtained by freelance journalist Jeremy Bigwood under the US Freedom of Information Act, and published by Eva

Golinger.[15] The US government is exposed to the charge that it is cynical in its use of the language of democracy. If Venezuela were an isolated case, we might overlook it as an aberration, the activities of rogue elements within the US power structure. But the evidence is overwhelming that the US employed similar tactics against countries in its so-called 'backyard' such as Nicaragua and Haiti. In fact, the catalogue of US military interventions in, and covert subversion of, other sovereign states reveals a global agenda.[16]

Is there a viable alternative to this geo-political interventionism that embitters the victims of those who use the language of democracy as a camouflage to favour the elites? The quest for reform should begin by asking why the USA is willing to manipulate the concept of democracy. Democrats are supposed to respect the views of the majority. But for the US, at times, democracy appears to be conditional on the privatisation of land and resource rents. Abraham Lincoln believed that American democracy was "the last best hope of earth".[17] but the American Dream needs serious reconsideration.[18]

It would be wrong, however, to hold the US solely responsible for bad neighbourliness. As we have noted, citing the President of Brazil, countries that want to change need to accept responsibility for the alleviation of their own prob-lems. In the case of Venezuela, the socialist paradigm is of little use to the people. It was well tested—and abandoned—in the 20th century. So why wave the red flag under the beak of the American eagle other than for vicarious mischief?[19]

As for the crude, private version of property rights in land, which the US holds sacred—reform can be articulated through the language of freedom. If Chávez had announced not land reform, but tax reform, Washington would have had difficulty in justifying its plots against the government in Caracas. If Chávez had championed the principle that people should pay for the benefits they receive, his words would have been straight out of Adam Smith's The Wealth of Nations. Smith explained that landowners should fund the public services that gave value to their estates. How could Washington subvert Adam Smith's agenda? Publicly, it couldn't. The sophisticated outcome of this alternative agenda would be the socialisation of rent and the privatisation of wages and profits. That is what we may call social capitalism. This is not a hybrid (a pastiche of existing political doctrines), but a unique philosophy of social organisation designed to liberate the individual and protect the common good.

A redeveloping country that adopted this doctrine would ensure a flow of funds that would free it of the need to negotiate—from weakness—for finance on the terms of the Washington Consensus. Such a country would self-fund its redevelopment in a post-colonial form, and would therefore achieve the sovereignty that is now possessed in name only. If Venezuela pioneered this financial policy, it would emancipate the poor without impoverishing the working rich. That is the 'silver bullet' available to governments everywhere in the world today. There is no other way to consign poverty to history.

Epilogue

Pauperisation: the Process beyond Poverty

In future, we need to burrow down much more deeply into the phenomenon of poverty. Its nature has changed: because the material achievements of the past 30 years in some redeveloping countries have been offset by a steep rise in what we call pauperisation. This condition touches everyone on both sides of the income divide. Here we present this concept, the evidence for which is elaborated at length elsewhere.[1]

In 1994 the United Nations argued that the world had to move beyond national security—the notion that was narrowly concerned with territorial imperatives, the need to guard against external aggressors. We now required "another profound transition in thinking—from nuclear security to human security".[2] This was defined by four characteristics. Human security is a universal concern, the components of which were interdependent. Human security was easier to ensure through early prevention, and was people-centred. "It is concerned with how people live and breathe in a society, how freely they exercise their many choices, how much access they have to market and social opportunities—and whether they live in conflict or in peace."[3]

This was a restatement of the human rights doctrine embodied in the UN's foundation document. But since 1948, people's need for security has been systematically abused. Insecurity has deepened in the rich nations (most notably in the Anglo-American zone), let alone in those countries populated by people living on less than $1-a-day.

- In the UK the geographical maldistribution of wealth and poverty since 1970, explained elsewhere,[4] has been confirmed by exhaustive examination of official statistics.

The historic trend is away from equality. Wealthy areas (and classes and individuals) have tended to become disproportionately wealthier. An increasing polarisation is driving spatially deeper wedges between rich and poor, fragmenting communities to the point where, in some city locations, over half of all households are deemed to be 'breadline poor'.[5]

- In the USA, tens of millions of families survive only because mothers seek employment to cover the cost of the mortgage. Real wages have been falling since about 1975. This decline in material standards is reflected in the erosion in the American citizen's constitutional 'right' to happiness.[6]

According to one estimate, between 1979 and 2004 the pre-tax incomes of the top 1% of Americans had increased by $664bn ($600,000 per family), an increase of 43%. The lower 80% of families were worse off by $7,000 in income per family (a 14% loss) —with the trend continuing to widen the gap.[7]

We can see that the capitalist model does not provide for sustainable growth; nor does it deliver equity between individuals or classes. But the problem that we wish to highlight is this: the material deprivation index fails to capture the full horror that follows the separation of people from their natural environment.

Pauperisation can be observed in the way that some indigenous peoples find themselves marooned on modern versions of reservations. Their culture began to implode the moment they were separated from ancient land rights. Their lives ruptured from traditional cultural forms of activity, they seek solace in drugs, alcohol and other self-destructive behaviour. The material welfare made available by govern-ment is no protection against the trauma that results from personal and group detachment from their ecological niche. Poverty slides into the pauperisation of personality and community.

According to the UN, we would all benefit from a general mobi-lisation in favour of 'human security',

By responding to the threat of global poverty travelling across international borders in the form of drugs, HIV/AIDS, climate change, illegal migration and terrorism.[8]

But the UN's notion of human security fails to address the proc-ess of pauperisation. Furthermore, even the need for security can-not be achieved if we do not restore the role of land in our lives.

Pauperisation encompasses material, psychic and spiritual forms of deprivation. A country's per capita income can rise—suggesting it is reducing poverty—while at the same time the welfare of the population may deteriorate. The growth in national income can be associated (as we have seen most-tragically in post-Soviet Russia) with a desperate deterioration in the quality of people's lives.

The concept of potential is crucial to a consideration of what we mean by pauperisation. It is the measure of achievements unrealised. It reminds us of how we could all enjoy peace and the economics of abundance. But abundance does not allude to material satiation. It refers to that contentment which comes with the state of liberty—of not being subjected to arbitrary restraints imposed by others, and of being equipped to challenge oneself to achieve personal goals.

The UN's notion of human security is underpinned by a doctrine of 'human rights' that pauperises people in the rich as well as in the poor regions of the world. In England and Wales, for example, one in three children still live in poverty.[9] This is relative poverty: it is impossible to compare the poor children of England to the poor children of Malawi. But this poverty contributes to the collective sense of a pervasive social malaise which is now spawning acts of desperation. These include the self-destructive acts of suicide bombers who are reared in families that do not lack material resources, but who experience a profound sense of deprivation and alienation.

We do not claim that fiscal reform will be the instant answer to religious fanatics or corporate bullies. We do claim that the agenda set out in Part 3 provides the framework for a new sense of justice in our relationships both with each other and with Earth. This fiscal agenda assumes critical importance when we realise that narrowly defined poverty, by itself, cannot explain the global crises that are converging in the 21st century.

The billion people who suffer the $1-a-day material deprivation constitute but one of four inter-related global challenges. The other three are:

• Terrorism. No corner on earth is free of this brand of violence, which is used as a tool of politics by other means. Is force really the optimum way to address the causes that inspire what President George W Bush called "the axis of evil"?

- The eco-crisis. All nations agree that nature is, now, about to wreak revenge on humanity. We will all be affected by climatic shifts. Should we allow the polluters to set the terms for reducing that damage?
- International trade. When two billion people from the ex-socialist East arrived in the market economy, the demand for protectionism was resurrected in the West. That demand will be heightened as the global economy dives into a recession.[10] Should trade be framed to suit the corporate rent-seekers?

The correct reforms will not be adopted without a full understanding of the facts by people with open minds. The price of failure is beyond our present comprehension.

What You Can Do

Solving the Perpetual Debt Crisis

Once it is privatised, the rent of land and of nature's resources is converted from public value to private debt. Its
essence remains: rent is the product of cooperative effort,
institutionally separated from private incomes through the social
rules of the marketplace. But it is transformed from benign social
surplus, available to fund the secular arts and spiritual life (among
other things), into a legal force that tears culture apart. Rent becomes a debt—a transfer payment, as economists put it—that is
owed by the majority to the privileged minority. The owners of
land interpose themselves between people and nature, causing
the implosion of society in a thousand and one ways.

The community of nations is in need of a period of social
renewal, so that people can see the need for changes to property
rights and public finance policies. What will encourage such
reforms? Pessimistically, the Asian Development Bank notes that
"the most successful redist-ributions" of land take place after
wars, citing South Korea and Taiwan. "Is the redistribution of land
possible in less extreme circumstances?", it asks. "[T]he answer to
this question may well be 'No'".[1]

Wars, driven by the desire for territorial aggrandisement, were intrinsic to past Ages of Unenlightenment. Must we resign our-selves to the prospect that future reforms can only follow destruc-tive conflicts? Or should we hope that, by democratic debate, and by showing that everyone gains from tax-and-tenure reform, en-lightened people will reclaim their birthright without others first having to die?

Neo-colonised countries that wish to redevelop, need to take control of the agenda if they wish to determine their fate. Westerners can help, and a good starting point for them is the recognition that a new approach is needed to debt cancellation. Relief from the debts that cripple whole societies must be sought by new means.

We need to start with a deeper understanding of the nature of this debt, as defined by the United Nations. The UN recommends that, in national accounts, balance sheets should have entries for buildings, machinery and vehicles, but should exclude land.[2] Why? The UN correctly defines land as a non-produced asset. This means that the money paid for its use is a simple transfer of income from one person or group to another. Rent, when privatised, does not represent an exchange of value-for-value.

For so long as that form of debt hangs around the budgets of nations, it must impede evolution towards communities that are balanced in personal health, wealth and social welfare.

The debt cancellation agenda, therefore, should switch its em-phasis from debts owed to banks to the far larger debt—one that otherwise exists in perpetuity—which is paid to those who liter-ally own the country and claim the legal right to extract a nation's rents.

We need a new and different campaign to consign poverty to history. To support the goodwill of individual reformers, that campaign should be endorsed by governments that genuinely wish to see the redevelopment of their post-colonial societies. The starting point should be a move for change to the constitutions and declarations of human rights that inspire people; which mobilise moral authority behind popular consensus for change. In particular, attention now needs to focus on the endorsement of amendments to the UN Universal Declaration of Human Rights.

We saw in chapter 7 that the UN's version of human rights does not outlaw this most pernicious of all debts.[3] The Universal Declaration of Human Rights, by its act of omission, permits rent-takers to hold nations to ransom. Agreement is needed between member countries to modify the Declaration. Clauses need to be amended to embed the principles of justice. The amended Declaration would then help reformers to revise the laws of their own land.

The International Union for Land Value Taxation (the IU), the publishers of this book, has launched a global campaign to petition the UN to secure amendments to Articles 3 and 29 of the Declaration, taking the form of additional wordings shown here in italics:

Article 3 Everyone has the right to life, liberty and security of person, *the enjoyment of which is dependent on the right of access to land. Land may be accessed indirectly, by sharing in the benefit of the enhanced use of land that accrues within a community when use rights are assigned to others. The right to land will be satisfied when that sharing is equitable and proportionate to the benefit.*

Article 29 (1) Everyone has duties to the community in which alone the free and full development of his personality is possible. *The life of the community is reliant on the performance of those duties, principal among which is the payment to the*

community of the value of the land benefits received from it....
This formulation—sharing in the benefits—has two virtues.

- It does not require the forced appropriation of anyone's land holdings. Security of possession would continue, tied to the obligation to pay for the benefits that the possessors receive by virtue of holding land.
- Benefits may take monetary and non-monetary form. So a land-holding jurisdiction could employ a land use policy that does not entail the payment of rent for the use of land, if it so wished. Such cases are exceptional—we have cited the case of the Kalahari Desert Bushmen—but they must be respected. For we are specifying a universal right; which means that it must be applicable to societies at any stage of 'development'.

This formulation of the rights and obligations of each and every one of us offers the most powerful single tool for abolishing involuntary poverty.

The amended Articles are the logical culmination of decisions that have already been made by the UN (see box facing). If adopted by the United Nations General Assembly, and enforced by member countries, the Earth ethic enshrined in the Universal Declaration of Human Rights would transform the document into the Declaration of Universal Human Rights. This formulation delivers the power, in principle, to secure people's natural right to life and liberty. We believe that the amended Declaration would inspire governments to reform their tax codes—making it possible to unburden those who work for their living, by collecting revenue from the community's natural financial fund—as the prelude to consigning poverty to history.

You are invited to go to www.UNpetition.net to sign and sup-

"The Common Heritage of Mankind"

THE United Nations has begun to elucidate the philosophy of land rights that the IU recommends, starting with The Third United Nations Convention on the Law of the Sea (1982). This declares that

> the area of the seabed and ocean floor and the subsoil thereof, beyond the limits of national jurisdiction, as well as its resources, are the common heritage of mankind, the exploration and exploitation of which shall be carried out for the benefit of mankind as a whole, irrespective of the geographical location of states....

And UN-Habitat, which is charged with identifying solutions to meet people's need for shelter, specifies the means for sharing urban land rent. Land, it declares,

> cannot be treated as an ordinary asset, controlled by individuals and subject to the pressures and inefficiencies of the market. Private land ownership is also a principal instrument of accumulation and concentration of wealth and therefore contributes to social injustice; if unchecked, it may become a major obstacle in the planning and implementation of development schemes. The provision of decent dwellings and healthy conditions for the people can only be achieved if land is used in the interests of society as a whole. Public control of land use is therefore indispensable... (emphasis added).

It adds, that to

> exercise such control effectively....suitable instruments [are required] for assessing the value of land and transferring to the community, inter alia through taxation, the unearned increment resulting from changes in use, or public investment or decisions, or due to the general growth of the community.*

* The UN Conference on Human Settlements (Habitat I), Vancouver, May 31-June 11, 1976, Conference Report, Preamble to Agenda Item 10.

port the petition, and to invite others to join you. A free digital copy of The Silver Bullet may be downloaded and forwarded to those who wish to understand why tax-and-tenure reform is imperative if we are to render mass poverty and territorial conflicts obsolete.[4] Governments and representative organisations in politics and civil society are invited to endorse the campaign and support the petition, and to make their own representations to members of the General Assembly.

The need for inter-governmental initiatives has been recognised by people like Gordon Brown, Britain's Prime Minister. He now realises that the Millennium Development Goals are not being achieved—"it is already clear that our pace is too slow, our direction too uncertain, our vision at risk".[5] He has assembled a coalition of government leaders and multinational corporations to convene at a UN-sponsored conference in 2008 to address the deepening poverty in Africa. But without a comprehensive understanding of the causes of poverty, such initiatives will go the way of previous gatherings, where hand-wringing was not followed by action proportionate to the problem or its root causes.

The peoples of Africa and the other neo-colonised regions do not need the kind of aid that reduces them to dependent clients. They can enjoy cultural and economic renewal by funding out of their own resources their capital-intensive needs. This transformation would unite the world's citizenry through a declared common stake in its natural home. A fairer, richer, international community united to address the global crises that now beset us all on Earth.

References

Poverty:
Redefining Rights & Obligations

1. The measure of success of the Welfare State is the abolition of the appalling injustices of the 19th century industrial economy. While it does have achievements to its credit, these have been purchased at the expense of personal liberty, the evidence for which is documented in Harrison (2006a). The flow of income was supposed to be from the rich to the poor; in reality, it has been in the opposite direction.
2. Estimate by Alistair Darling, Britain's Chancellor of the Exchequer in Gordon Brown's administration (Barriaux (2007)).
3. Brogan (2007)
4. Stiglitz (2007) pp. 140-141
5. UN Development Programme (1994) p. 26
6. United Nations (2000) p. 20
7. UN Development Programme (1999)
8. Sala-i-Martin (2007) p. 25
9. Chen and Ravallion (2004) p. 20. Their projections do not take into account the prospect of a global depression around 2010 which has been forecast by the present author (Harrison (2005)), which would cancel much of the progress made by China and India in recent years.
10. Sala-i-Martin (2007) p. 24
11. Bardhan (2007) p. 3, who adds: "Paradoxically, the potential for unrest may be greater in the currently-booming urban areas, where the real-estate bubble could break. Global recession could ripple through the excess-capacity industries and financially-shaky public banks... [U]rban unrest may be more difficult to contain".
12. Lewis (1983)
13. Asian Development Bank [ADB] (2007) p. 12, box 2.2

14. Kanbur (2000)
15. ADB (2007) Loc.cit.
16. Giles (2007)
17. World Bank (2005) p. 99, emphasis added.

I "The Most Important Economist in the World"

1. Passell (1993). The New York Times reporter wrote that "Sach's brand of 'shock therapy' has worked elsewhere. And there is good reason to believe that Russia's future will turn on how well its leaders learn the catechism of change that he has worked so hard to promulgate".
2. We allude to the concept of pauperisation, which is introduced in the Epilogue. This process is elaborated elsewhere (Harrison (forthcoming)).
3. Sachs (2005) p. 131. This section is based on Sachs' account in chapter 7 of The End of Poverty, and the present author's work in Russia in the ten years following the departure of Sachs for other climes.
4. Id. p. 135
5. Id. p. 148
6. Loc. cit.
7. This model, with its emphasis on monetarist policies and the privatisation of public assets, was foreshadowed in Latin America in the 1980s. It became known as the Washington Consensus because of the strategies that were agreed between, and implemented by, the US Government, the IMF and the World Bank. For a critical evaluation of the theoretical underpinnings of this consensus, see Stiglitz (2002).
8. Sachs (2005) pp. 143-144
9. The historical analogies—such as the robber barons who plundered the natural resources of the United States—were available to analysts who were interested in learning the lessons of the past.
10. Sachs (2000) p. 146. Six years after his departure from Moscow, Sachs reassessed his work in Russia in these terms: "[M]y actual influence on events was essentially zero". But, based on many interviews with Russians, from the Federal Duma down through local governments and to people on the streets, I can confirm that citizens attributed significant influence to the role played by Jeffrey Sachs. For another recent account of the Sachs project in Russia, see Klein (2007).
11. Banerjee and Iyer (2005) p. 15
12. Id. p. 26
13. Sachs (2005) p. 183

References

14. Loc. cit.
15. Harrison (1994) pp. 199-204
16. Harrison (forthcoming)
17. Vaid (2006)
18. Selja (2006a). Scrapping the Act made it possible to release large tracts of land that had been locked up by the law. In Mumbai alone, the conservative estimate was that about 25,000 acres would become available for development in the metropolis.
19. Sachs (2006)
20. Collier (2005) pp. 41-42

2 Blame it on Nature

1. Sachs and Warner (1995) & (2001)
2. Sachs and Warner (2001) p. 828
3. Harrison (forthcoming)
4. This account of the resource curse is based on Collier (2007) chapter 3 & Collier and Hoeffler (2005).
5. For their modelling work, Collier and Hoeffler (2005) p. 17 added up rents for oil, gas, coal, lignite, bauxite, copper, iron, lead, nickel, phosphate, tin, zinc, silver and gold. They did not estimate the rents of urban land, which in many countries would constitute a significant proportion of the total of the rents of land and natural resources; or the rents, for example, from marine resources and the electromagnetic spectrum.
6. Acemoglu (2003) p. 29
7. Loc. cit.
8. Acemoglu, Johnson and Robinson (2001) p. 1
9. Id. pp. 23-24
10. Id. p. 27
11. Sachs and Warner (2001) p. 833
12. Iimi (2006) p. 4
13. Acemoglu, Johnson and Robinson (2002)
14. Id. p. 21
15. Acemoglu et al (2001) p. 4
16. Acemoglu et al (2002) p. 10. Cattle is the etymological origin of 'capital', an asset owned privately according to the earliest known societies.
17. Acemoglu et al (2001) p. 19
18. Id. p. 24
19. Id. p. 32
20. Temane (1980) p. 2
21. Id. p. 3

22. Id. p. 13
23. Loc. cit.
24. Id. p. 14
25. Stiglitz (2002) p. 39
26. Ibid.

3 A Theory of Corruption

1. Smith (1776) Book v, chapter 11, part 2, article 1, p. 370 of the Cannan edition
2. Mill (1891) p. 524
3. George (1879)
4. On continental Europe, two important theorists who favoured the community-sharing of rent were Herman-Henri Gossen and Leon Walras. Their writings are reviewed by Scornik Gerstein and Foldvary (forthcoming).
5. Miller (2000) p. 385
6. Marshall (1930) p. 445
7. Quoted in Miller (2000) p. 386
8. Narain (1971) p. 59, citing The Fifth Report to the House of Commons on the East India Affairs, vol. 1, Calcutta, 1917-18
9. Narain (1971) pp. 64-65
10. Id. p. 67
11. Jha (1971) p. 72
12. Id. p. 73
13. Id. p. 77
14. Marshall (1930) pp. 802-803
15. Id. p. 803
16. Schumpeter (1954) p. 769
17. Garrett Hardin, author of the controversial 'tragedy of the commons' thesis, employed this argument in relation to Henry George. Hardin "always thought it a shame that he [George] could not have been born two centuries earlier and laid out the ground rules for the development of the New World" (Andelson (1991) p. viii). Adam Smith, of course, was around two centuries earlier; but his proposal that the rent of land should form the basis of public spending was studiously ignored by the Founding Fathers of the United States.
18. UNFPA (2007)
19. Pei (2007)
20. Id. p. 3. Sales of land user rights by the government generated 580bn yuan in 2005. Bribes to local officials amounting to 10-20% of these revenues implies the privatisation of rent at an annual rate of 0.5-1.0% of GDP.
21. Shaikh (2007)

References

22. de Soto (1989) p. 18
23. The Economist (2006) & Field and Torero (2006)
24. Guha (2007)

4 South America: From Farm to *Favela*

1. Frankema (2006) & World Bank (2004). Frankema fails to distinguish between 'land inequality' (which relates to the distribution of physical space) and the unequal distribution of land's value. It is possible (say, for the sake of efficiency of production) to have the former, while at the same time securing the equalisation of the value of land through fiscal policy.
2. Lindert, Skoufias and Shapiro (2006) p. 14, box 3
3. World Bank (2004), cited in Frankema (2006) p. 3
4. Bolivia lost nearly 500,000 km² to Brazil in the dispute over rubber. Chile and Paraguay appropriated chunks of territory in order to procure their nitrates and petroleum.
5. Easterly (2006) p. 100, who provides a masterly summary of the land grab in Bolivia (pp. 99-101).
6. Spooner (1980)
7. Hoge (1980)
8. O'Shaughnessy (1980)
9. Asheshov (1980)
10. Sachs (2005) p. 92
11. Id. p. 89
12. Easterly (2006) p. 100
13. Simons (1984)
14. Bolivia's peasants were made to fund the urban infrastructure that was enjoyed by absentee land owners who preferred life in the cities. Between 1960 and 1964, for example, although the rural sector employed almost 60% of the labour force, it received just 0.7-1.9% of all public investments. Investment in the urban infrastructure raised the value of urban land, while life in the rural villages was impoverished.
15. Sachs (2005) p. 108, figure 3
16. Weitzman (2005)
17. Wheatley (2007)

5 Asia: the Role of Mega-Projects

The Silver Bullet

1. Harrison (forthcoming)
2. This unjust outcome of public revenue policy consequently reaches deep into the whole financial system. For example, the secondary market for mortgage-backed securities means that the wealthy also hold the debt of those who borrow to acquire housing. Government bonds are also held by the wealthy, receiving interest payments, the revenue for which must be raised by taxing the wealth-producing segments of society. Governments have reduced the marginal tax rates on the highest incomes, which means that the wealthy have more disposable income to 'invest' in government debt, in the stock market and in real estate.
3. Harrison (2006a)
4. Selja (2006a) & (2006b)
5. Harrison (1983) & (2005)
6. Acharya (2007)
7. ADB (2007) p. 86
8. Lam (2000) pp. 327-328
9. Sun Yat-Sen lost power in 1911. He returned to power in 1922, but the implementation of land and tax reform was postponed because of the actions by warlords who controlled parts of China's interior. Before his death, however, Sun commissioned Dr. Ludwig Schrameier to prepare the administration of the principles contained in San Min Chu I. Schrameier had used the rent-as-public-revenue policy in the German colony of Kiao Chan (Tsing Tao). During the 17 years in which he administered the colony, rapid progress was made in funding the infrastructure of the seaport, a progress that ended with the Japanese occupation in 1916. Peterson and Tseng (2000) p. 368 conclude that, "For all practical purposes, the system may be, and, indeed was, regarded as the essential realisation of the single-tax doctrine of Henry George. This was conceded by Schrameier himself, although he claimed not to have been influenced by Georgism directly, but by the practical necessities of administering the territory".
10. The data in the table on p. 98 is for 2005. China's GDP in that year was the result of the remarkable growth over the previous 20 years. This, therefore, misrepresents the gap (which was even wider) between the incomes of the two economies during the three decades between 1949 and the market reforms that the Communist Party began to initiate in 1979.
11. Sachs (2005) p. 160
12. Id. p. 161
13. Over the decade to 2017, fifteen Chinese cities are expected to build 1,700 km of underground lines and urban light railways. This explosive growth in infrastructure will shift an enormous increase in state-funded urban rents into the pockets of leaseholders rather than the public purse.
14. Sachs (2005) p. 167
15. Ibid.
16. Id. p. 168

References

17. Harrison (2006b). A free download is available from <www.iea.org.uk/record.jsp?ID=307&type=book>.

6 Africa: the Great Plunder

1. Mayson (2004)
2. UN Development Programme (1994) p. 46
3. Ibid.
4. Ibid.
5. Ibid.
6. This did not exonerate the Zimbabwe government entirely. Much of the land that had been purchased from the whites went to cronies of Zanu-PF, the ruling party, and much of that land was not used productively.
7. Stiglitz (2002) pp. 80-81
8. Russell (2007)
9. McGreal (2007a)
10. Christensen (2007)
11. Harrison (2006a)
12. Global Witness (2007) p. 9
13. Alaska Permanent Fund Corporation <www.apfc.org/alaska/dividend/dividendPrgrm.cfm>

7 Governance & the UN

1. Dillinger (1991)
2. Id. p. 4
3. Harrison (2006a) p. 208
4. Locke (1690) chapter 5
5. Jensen (1970)
6. In Britain, for example, with its Welfare State and commitment to the human rights championed by the UN, an estimated 50,000 people die prematurely every year because of the impact of the tax regime. The estimate is by the late Dr. George Miller, who was a member of Britain's Medical Research Council's Senior Clinical Scientific Staff, and Professor of Epidemiology at the University of London Queen Mary and Westfield College (see Miller (2003)).
7. Difficulties with the concept of the right to work in human rights legislation are reviewed in Blake (2002) pp. 144-145. See also Blake (2000).
8. Dorling at al (2007). The authors found that the wealth gap had increased

over the previous 40 years—the better part of the life of the Welfare State, which employed progressive taxation. What the authors called the 'breadline poor' households had increased over this period, peaking at 27% in 2001.

9. Dillinger (1991) para. 7 [a]
10. Jensen (1970) p. 66. Galloway was a conservative who did not want independence from Britain. Jensen, pp. 12-13, explained that Galloway "sought to tighten the bonds between the colonies and the mother country and thus to consolidate the power and bulwark the position of the colonial aristocracy".
11. Warden (2001) p. 82. Neo-colonised countries are told that freehold property rights are essential to attract foreign investors. The Dutch tulip industry, however, has invested in Ethiopia because it needs the sun and, in return, has no problem with paying the solar rents to the people of Ethiopia. The Ethiopian Investment Agency <www.investethiopia.org> provides information on leasehold rents which vary according to location.
12. Jupp (2001) p. 132

8 Settlers & the Land Tax

1. Kane, Holmes and O'Grady (2007)
2. Cruden (1986)
3. Phang (2000) chapter 20
4. Harrison (2006b) pp. 87-94
5. Noticias Históricas,Políticas y Estadísticas de las Provincias Unidas del Río de la Plata, London, 1825, pp. 294-296, quoted in Scornik Gerstein (2000) p. 50.
6. Scornik Gerstein (2000) p. 60. Although instructed by the Ministry of Economy to deliver a report only on rural taxation, Scornik Gerstein's document also explained the benefits of taxing urban land, along with compensating reductions in other taxes. This report is reprinted in Scornik Gerstein (2007).
7. McLean (1997)
8. McLean (2005) p. 2. Rejecting the thesis by Sachs and Warner (1995), McLean adds, p. 13, that "consideration must be given [to] policies and institutions, especially those influencing access to resources and the distribution of rents".
9. Broadberry and Irwin (2006) p. 12 (p. 262)
10. Huberman (2004) table 7
11. This analysis, of course, fails to factor in the human and cultural costs to the indigenous people who were displaced or otherwise affected by the arrival of the settlers.
12. McLean (2004) p. 19

References

13. Id. p. 16, note 32
14. New Zealand beat Australia to the land tax principle, which it adopted in 1841. In 1855, the province of New Plymouth introduced a rate on the "fair value of land exclusive of the value of improvements" (Keall (2000)).
15. Queensland adopted A Bill To Declare the Natural Law Relating to the Acquisition and Ownership of Private Property in 1890, drafted by Sir Samuel Griffith, who was later to serve as Chief Justice. The definitions of terms such as land and rent remain models of clarity. The Bill is reproduced in Jupp (1997) appendix. For an assessment of the influence of Henry George on Australian fiscal policy, see Forster (2000).
16. Herps (1988) p. 4
17. Quoted in Forster (2000) p. 408
18. Harrison (1983) chapter 18 & (2005) chapter 13
19. Kavanagh (2007) p. 21

9 Social Capitalism

1. IMF (2005) pp. 14-16
2. Dunkley (1990)
3. Personal communication from Godfrey Dunkley to the author, June 5, 2007.
4. Lamont (2007)
5. Russell (2007)
6. Foster (2007)
7. Dhanendra Kumar, India's representative on the World Bank's board, quoted in Guha and Yee (2007).
8. Bardhan (2007) p. 2
9. Id. p. 3
10. Ramesh and Jha (2007)
11. Ramesh (2007)
12. The erosion of India's commons continues unrelentingly. In one southern state (Karnataka), for example, encroachment shifts power from commoners to large land owners. In 1990, the state government amended the Land Revenue Act (1964) to allow for the enclosure of 725,000 acres, or 5.5% of the state's remaining land (Robinson (2004) p. 3). A year later, over 1 million applications were made for the regularisation of over 2.5m acres of encroached land, about 20% of the state's commons. The land grabbing included the privatisation of small reservoirs and sacred groves.
13. Golinger (2007) p. 48
14. Vidal and Borger (2007)
15. Golinger (2007), with further documentation on <www.venezuelafoia. info>.

16. Blum (2003)
17. Neely (1995). Lincoln wrote: "My dream is of a place and a time where America will once again be seen as the last best hope of earth".
18. The motivation behind US intervention in other countries was illustrated in Novgorod, the ancient capital of Russia. The present author, with colleagues including Ronald Banks and Ted Gwartney, was involved in arranging for the city's Land Tax to be modernised, with updated assessments based on site rents. Before implementation, however, USAID conducted its own study, supplied the mayor's administration with free computer hardware, and secured agreement that the Western property tax (which reduces the charge on land values by transferring the burden on to buildings) should be adopted.
19. The Chávez programme of new-style socialism reintroduced old-style effects reminiscent of the Soviet era: despite the oil boom, which increased rent revenues enormously, food shortages appeared through-out the country. Milk, eggs and sugar all but vanished from shops, with supplies rationed and hands stamped to prevent cheating (Carroll 2007).

Pauperisation:
the Process beyond Poverty

1. Harrison (forthcoming)
2. UN Development Programme (1994) p. 22. The concept of human security is summarised in UN Development Programme (1999) p. 36, box 1.3.
3. Id. p. 23
4. Harrison (2006a). The drugs dependency in the West is not the direct product of poverty, but of the pauperisation of culture: discontent with life creates the need to fill the void with escapist potions of one kind or another. As it happens, in relation to narcotics, this creates a demand that some countries like Colombia and Afghanistan can tap, to make up for the deficiencies in incomes from socially benign forms of economic activity. The resort to cultivating cocaine leads to organised crime, or organised terror, which are two variants of the violence unleashed by pauperisation.
5. Dorling et al (2007) & Thomas and Dorling (2007)
6. Harrison (2006a) chapter 12
7. Summers (2007)
8. UN Development Programme (1994) p. 24
9. Magadi and Middleton (2007)
10. Harrison (2005)

References

What You Can Do:
Solving the Perpetual Debt Crisis

1. ADB (2007) p. 81, note 90
2. United Nations (1993)
3. In the ancient world, debt cancellation practices by high priests and princes found expression in the Bible as the Jubilee (Leviticus, chapter 25). For a modern interpretation of the Jubilee, see Hudson (1994) & (1999) & (2002).
4. For an account of how to implement public charges on land values, see UN-Habitat's Global Land Tool Network at <www.unhabitat.org/categories.asp?catid=503>.
5. Eaglesham (2007)

Bibliography

Acemoglu, Daron (2003): 'Root causes: a historical approach to assessing the role of institutions in economic development', Finance & Development, Washington DC, World Bank, June

Acemoglu, Daron, Simon Johnson and James A Robinson (2001): 'The Colonial Origins of Comparative Development: An Empirical Investigation', American Economic Review, 91

Acemoglu, Daron, Simon Johnson and James A Robinson (2002): An African Success Story: Botswana, CEPR Discussion Paper No. 3219

Acharya, Shankar (2007): Can India Grow without Bharat?, New Delhi: Academic Foundation

Andelson, RV (ed.) (1991): Commons Without Tragedy, London: Shepheard-Walwyn

Andelson, RV (ed.) (2000): Land-Value Taxation Around the World, 3rd edition, Oxford: Blackwell

Asheshov, Nicholas (1980): 'Gung-ho terrorism rides high on cocaine', The Sunday Times, August 10

Asian Development Bank (2007): Key Indicators 2007, Manila: ADB, 38

Banerjee, Abhijit, and Lakshmi Iyer (2005): 'History, institutions and economic performance: the legacy of colonial land tenure systems in India' <www.bu.edu/econ/ied/neudc/papers/Iyer-Final2.pdf>

Bardhan, Pranab (2007): 'Inequality in India and China: Is Globalisation to Blame?' YaleGlobal Online <yaleglobal.yale.edu/article.print?id=9819>

Barriaux, Marianne (2007): 'Child poverty deadline will be missed, warn charities', The Guardian, October 10

Benjamin, Solomon (2001): 'Globalization's impact on local government', UN-Habitat Debate 7

Blair, David (2007): 'Geldof and Bono criticise G8 leaders for "betrayal" of Africa', Daily Telegraph, June 9

Blake LL (2000): 'Public Charges for the Use of Inter-Planetary Resources', Geophilos, Autumn, 00(1)

Blake LL (2002): 'How to Approach Rent Through Rights', Geophilos, Spring 02(1)

Blum, William (2003): Killing Hope: US Military & CIA Interventions Since World War II, London: Zed Books

Bibliography

Broadberry, Stephen, and Douglas A Irwin (2006): 'Lost Exceptionalism? Comparative Income and Productivity in Australia and the UK, 1861-1948', Economic Record, 83

Brogan, Benedict (2007): 'Welfare pledge will take Cameron into Labour's territory', Daily Mail, October 16

Carroll, Rory (2007): 'Venezuelans queue for food despite oil boom', The Guardian, November 14

Chen, Shaohua, and Martin Ravaillon (2004): 'How have the world's poorest fared since the early 1980s?', Development Research Group, World Bank Policy Working Paper No. 3341 <www.worldbank.org/research/povmonitor/MartinPapers/>

Christensen, John (2007): 'Dirty money flows distort our economy and corrupt democracy', The Guardian, May 30

Collier, Paul (2007a): The Bottom Billion: Why the Poorest Countries are Failing and What Can Be Done About It, Oxford: Oxford University Press

Collier, Paul (2007b): 'The bottom billion bite back', The Sunday Times, July 1

Collier, Paul, and Anke Hoeffler (2005): 'Democracy and Resource Rents' <users.ox.ac.uk/~econpco>

Commission for Africa (2005): Our Common Interest, London: Penguin

Cruden, Gordon M (1986): Land Compensation and Valuation Law in Hong Kong, Singapore: Butterworth

Davis, Mike (2006): 'Haussmann in the Tropics' <world-information.org/wio/readme/992003309/1154965269>

de Ferranti, David M, et al (2004): Inequality in Latin America. Breaking with History?, Washington DC: World Bank Latin American and Caribbean Studies

de Soto, Hernando (1989): The Other Path: the Invisible Revolution in the Third World, New York: Harper and Row

Dillinger, William (1991): Urban Property Tax Reform: Guidelines and Recommendations, Washington DC: World Bank

Dorling, Daniel, et al (2007): Poverty, Wealth and Place in Britain 1968 to 2005, York: Joseph Rowntree Foundation

Dunkley, Godfrey (1990): That All May Live, Johannesburg: A Whyte Publishers

Dwyer, Terry (2003): 'The Taxable Capacity of Australian Land and Resources', Australian Tax Forum, 18(1)

Eaglesham, Jean (2007): 'Brown unveils global anti-poverty drive', Financial Times, August 1

Easterly, William (2006): The White Man's Burden, Oxford: Oxford University Press

Economist, The (2006): 'Of Property and Poverty', August 26-September 1

Field, Erica, and Maximo Torero (2006): 'Do Property Titles Increase Credit Access Among the Urban Poor? Evidence from a Nationwide Titling Program'. Available at <http://www.economics.harvard.edu/faculty/field/papers_field>.

Forster, Douglas (2000): 'Australia', in Andelson (2000)

Foster, Peter (2007): 'India will only be free when it has banished poverty, says PM', Daily Telegraph, August 16

Frankema, EHP (2006): 'The colonial origins of inequality: exploring the causes and consequences of land distribution', Groningen Growth and Development Centre, University of Groningen, Research Memorandum GD-81 <www.ggdc.nl/pub/gd81.pdf>

Gaffney, Mason, and Fred Harrison (1994): The Corruption of Economics, London: Shepheard-Walwyn

George, Henry (1879): Progress and Poverty, New York: Robert Schalkenbach Foundation, 1992

Giles, Christ (2007): 'World Bank makes farming priority in drive on poverty', Financial Times, October 20

Global Witness (2007): Oil Revenue Transparency: A Strategic Component of US Energy Security and Anti-Corruption Policy, London: Global Witness

Golinger, Eva (2007): The Chávez Code: Cracking US Intervention in Venezuela, London: Pluto Press

Goodland, Robert (2007): 'How to aid destruction', The Guardian, October 23

Greenstein, Rosalind, and Yesim Sungu-Eryilmaz (2007): 'Community Land Trusts: A solution for permanently affordable housing', Landlines, Cambridge, MA: Lincoln Institute of Land Policy, January

Guha, Krishna (2007): 'Tackling poverty a priority for Zoellick', Financial Times, October 11

Guha, Krishna, and Amy Yee (2007): 'World Bank loans to India climb 170%', Financial Times, July 6

Harrison, Fred (1983): The Power in the Land: An Inquiry into Unemployment, the Profits Crisis and Land Speculation, London: Shepheard-Walwyn

Harrison, Fred (1994): 'The Georgist Paradigm', in Mason Gaffney and Fred Harrison, The Corruption of Economics, London: Shepheard-Walwyn

Harrison, Fred (2005): Boom Bust: House Prices, Banking and the Depression of 2010, London: Shepheard-Walwyn

Harrison, Fred (2006a): Ricardo's Law: House Prices and the Great Tax Clawback Scam, London: Shepheard-Walwyn

Harrison, Fred (2006b): Wheels of Fortune, London: Institute of Economic Affairs. Free download from <www.iea.org.uk/files/upld-publication307pdf?.pdf>.

Harrison, Fred (forthcoming): The Pathology of Capitalism

Herps, MD (1988): 'Land Value Taxation in Australia and its potential for reforming our chaotic tax system', The Walsh Memorial Bequest Address, Macquarie University, May 27

Hiatt, Steven (2007): A Game as Old as Empire: The Secret World of Economic Hit Men and the Web of Global Corruption, San Francisco: Berrett-Koehler Publishers

Hoge, Warren (1980): 'Always a next time for the Bolivian army', New York Times, June 22

Bibliography

Huberman, Michael (2004): 'Working hours of the world unite? New international evidence of worktime, 1870-1913', Journal of Economic History, 64

Hudson, Michael (1994): 'Land Monopolization, Fiscal Crises and Clean Slate "Jubilee" Proclamations in Antiquity', in Michael Hudson, GJ Miller and Kris Feder: A Philosophy for a Fair Society, London: Shepheard Walwyn

Hudson, Michael (1999): 'The Economic Roots of the Jubilee', Bible Review, 15, February

Hudson, Michael (2002): 'Reconstructing the Origins of Interest-Bearing Debt and the Logic of Clean Slates', in Marc van de Mieroop and Michael Hudson (eds.): Debt and Economic Renewal in the Ancient Near East, Bethesda: CDL Press

Iimi, Atsushi (2006): 'Did Botswana escape from the Resource Curse?', Washington DC, IMF Working Paper 06/138 <www.sarpn.org.za/documents/d0002105/IMF_ Botswana_Iimi_Jun2006.pdf>

IMF (2005): Public Investment and Fiscal Policy—Lessons from the Pilot Country Studies <www.imf.org/external/np/pp/eng/2005/040105a.pdf>

Jacoby, Hanan G (2000): 'Access to markets and the benefits of rural roads', Economic Journal, 110

Jensen, Merrill (1970): The Articles of Confederation, Wisconsin: University of Wisconsin Press

Jha, JC (1971): 'History of land revenue in Chotanagpur (c. 1770-1830)', in Sharma (1971)

Jupp, Kenneth (1997): Stealing Our Land: The Law, Rent & Taxation, London: Othila Press

Jupp, Kenneth (2001): 'Constitutional Tenure & Taxation', Geophilos, Autumn 01(2)

Kanbur, R (2000): 'Income distribution and development', in AB Atkinson and F Bourguignon (eds.): Handbook of Income Distribution, Amsterdam: North-Holland

Kane, Tim, Kim R Holmes and Mary Anastasia O'Grady (2007): Index of Economic Freedom, Washington DC: The Heritage Foundation <www.heritage.org/ index/>

Kavanagh, Bryan (2007): Unlocking the Riches of Oz: A Case Study of the Social and Economic Costs of Real Estate Bubbles 1972-2006, Melbourne: Land Values Research Group

Keall, Robert D (2000): 'New Zealand', in Andelson (2000)

Klein, Naomi (2007): The Shock Doctrine, London: Allen Lane

Lam, Alven HS (2000): Chapter 19 in Andelson (2000)

Lamont, James (2007): 'Tutu warns on gulf between rich and poor', Financial Times, June 29

Leigh, David, and Rob Evans (2007): 'BAE accused of secretly paying £1bn to Saudi prince', The Guardian, June 7

Lewis, W Arthur (1983): Selected Economic Writings of W Arthur Lewis (M Gersovitz, ed.), New York: New York University Press

Lindert, Kathy, Emmanuel Skoufias and Joseph Shapiro (2006): Redistributing Income to the Poor and the Rich: Public Transfers in Latin America and the Caribbean, Washington DC: World Bank

Locke, John (1690): Second Treatise on Government, London: Oxford University Press, 1947

Maddison, Angus (1995): Monitoring the World Economy: 1820-1992, Paris: OECD

Magadi, Monica, and Sue Middleton (2007): Severe Child Poverty in the UK, London: Save the Children

Marshall, Alfred (1930): Principles of Economics, 8th edition, London: Macmillan

Mayson, David (2004): 'No funds—no land reform!', National Union of Metal Workers of South Africa <www.numsa.org.za>

McDowell, Christopher (1996): Understanding Impoverishment: The Consequences of Development-Induced Displacement, Providence: Berghahn Books

McGreal, Chris (2007a): 'Bakeries close their doors as collapse in wheat production adds to crisis', The Guardian, October 2

McGreal, Chris (2007b): '$5m honesty prize for Mozambican ex-leader', The Guardian, October 23

McLean, Ian (1997): Recovery from the 1890s Depression: Australia in an Argentine Mirror, Adelaide: University of Adelaide, CIES Seminar Paper, March

McLean, Ian (2004): Australian Economic Growth in Historical Perspective, Adelaide: University of Adelaide, Working Paper 2004-01

McLean, Ian (2005): Why Was Australia So Rich?, Adelaide: University of Adelaide, Working Paper 2005-11

Mill, John Stuart (1891): Principles of Political Economy, London: Routledge

Miller, George J (2000): On Fairness and Efficiency: The Privatisation of the Public Income Over the Past Millennium, Bristol: Policy Press

Miller, George J (2003): Dying for Justice, London: Centre for Land Policy Studies

Narain, VA (1971): 'Experiments in land revenue administration in Bengal (1765-1793)', in Sharma 1971

Neely, Mark E, Jr. (1995): The Last Best Hope of Earth: Abraham Lincoln and the Promise of America, Cambridge, MA: Harvard University Press

O'Shaughnessy, Hugh (1980): 'Probe urged into junta's drugs links', Financial Times, August 15

Page, Jeremy (2006): 'Indian slum population doubles in two decades', The Times, May 18

Passell, Peter (1993): 'Doctor Jeffrey Sachs, shock therapist', New York Times, June 27

Pei, Minxin (2007): Corruption Threatens China's Future, Washington DC: Carnegie Endowment for International Peace, Policy Brief 55

Peterson, VG, and Tseng Shiao (2000): Chapter 22 in Andelson (2000)

Pfeifer, Sylvia (2007): 'Lonrho breaks taboo with Zimbabwe venture', Sunday Telegraph, June 4

Phang, Sock-Yong (2000): 'Hong Kong and Singapore', in Andelson (2000)

Bibliography

Ramesh, Randeep (2007): 'Poor but defiant, thousands march on Delhi in fight for land rights', The Guardian, October 25

Ramesh, Randeep, and Sanjay Jha (2007): 'Indian government fears backlash as stock market hits record levels', The Guardian, October 16

Robinson, Elizabeth JZ (2004): Land Encroachment: India's Disappearing Common Lands, Centre for the Study of African Economies, Working Paper No. 228

Russell, Alec (2007a): 'Farmers struggling to survive without tools or training', Financial Times, May 25

Russell, Alec (2007b): 'Fenced in: why land reform in South Africa is losing its pace', Financial Times, November 6

Sachs, Jeffrey D (2000): 'Russia's tumultuous decade', The Washington Monthly <www.washingtonmonthly.com/boooks/2000/0003.sachs.html>

Sachs, Jeffrey D (2005): The End of Poverty: How We Can Make It Happen in Our Lifetime, London: Penguin

Sachs, Jeffrey D (2006): 'No "Magic Bullets" to End Poverty, Says Jeffrey Sachs', United Nations Integrated Regional Information Networks <www.globalpolicy.org/socecon/develop/2006/0320bullets.htm>

Sachs, Jeffrey, and Andrew M Warner (1995): Natural Resource Abundance and Economic Growth, Cambridge, MA: Harvard Institute for International Development, Development Discussion Paper 517a

Sachs, Jeffrey, and Andrew M Warner (2001): 'The curse of natural resources', European Economic Review, 45

Sala-i-Martin, Xavier (2006): 'The World Distribution of Income: Falling Poverty and...Convergence, Period', Quarterly Journal of Economics, 121, May

Sala-i-Martin, Xavier (2007): 'Global inequality fades as the global economy grows', in Tim Kane et al (2007)

Schumpeter, Joseph (1954): History of Economic Analysis, New York: Oxford University Press

Scornik Gerstein, Fernando (2000): 'Argentina', in Andelson (2000)

Scornik Gerstein, Fernando (2007): Tenencia de la Tierra para una sociedad mas justa, Buenos Aires: Instituto de Capacitación Económica

Scornik Gerstein, Fernando, and Fred Foldvary (forthcoming): The Marginalists and the Special Status of Land as a Factor of Production: Gossen, Wieser, Walras and Pareto

Selja, Kumari (2006a): Speech, Conference of Asia-Pacific Ministers, 'Housing and Human Settlements', Hyderabad, November 17

Selja, Kumari (2006b): Speech, Conference of Asia-Pacific Ministers, 'Housing and Human Settlements', New Delhi, December 15

Shaikh, Thair (2007): '26-year-old is China's richest person with £8.8bn fortune', The Guardian, October 9

Sharma, RS (1971): Land Revenue in India, Dehli: Motilal Banarsidass

Sheridan, Michael (2007): 'China's rich spark dissent from below', Sunday Times,

The Silver Bullet

October 21

Simons, Marlise (1983): 'Bolivian plot embarrasses the US', New York Times, July 17

Smith, Adam (1776): The Wealth of Nations, Chicago: University of Chicago Press, 1976

Soros, George (2004): The Bubble of American Supremacy, London: Phoenix

Spooner, Mary Helen (1980): 'Repression returns to Bolivia', Financial Times, July 31

Steiner, Henry J, Philip Alston and Ryan Goodman (2008): International Human Rights in Context: Law, Politics, Morals, Oxford: Oxford University Press, 3rd edition

Stiglitz, Joseph (2002): Globalization and its Discontents, Harmondsworth: Penguin

Stiglitz, Joseph (2007): Making Globalization Work: The Next Steps to Global Justice, London: Penguin

Summers, Lawrence (2007): 'Harness market forces to share prosperity', Financial Times, June 25

Tawney, RH (1932): Land and Labour in China, London: George Allen & Unwin

Temane, BK (1980): 'Land Tenure Systems and Land Reform in Botswana', Gaborone: Ministry of Local Government and Lands, paper delivered at World Congress on Land Policy, Lincoln Institute of Land Policy, Cambridge, MA, July 22-27

Thomas, Bethan, and Daniel Dorling (2007): Identity in Britain, Bristol: Policy Press

UN Development Programme (1994): Human Development Report, New York: United Nations

UN Development Programme (1999), Human Development Report, New York: United Nations <hdr.undp.org/reports/global/1999/en>

United Nations (1993): System of National Accounts 1993, New York: United Nations

United Nations (2000): Freedom from Want, New York: United Nations <www.un.org/millennium/sg/report/ch2.pdf>

Vidal, John (2007a): 'World Bank accused of razing Congo forests', The Guardian, October 4

Vidal, John (2007b): 'We said to them, "Come closer" but they said to us, "Go further back"', The Guardian, October 6

Vidal, John, and Julian Borger (2007): 'Brazil rejects Bush move on climate change talks', The Guardian, June 4

Warden, Gail (2001): 'The Ethiopian Model: Equal Land Rights in a Unique Social Development', Geophilos, Spring 01(1)

Weitzman, Hal (2005): 'Bolivian tension ahead as wealthy city girds itself for new president', Financial Times, December 29

Wheatley, Jonathan (2007): 'Farmers may reap the seeds of discontent', Financial

Bibliography

Times, June 20

Wightman, Andy (1999): Scotland: Land & Power, Edinburgh: Luath Press

Wightman, Andy (2001): 'Land Reform Draft Bill, Part 2—Community Right to Buy—An Analysis', Caledonia Centre for Social Development <www.andywightman.com/briefings/>

World Bank (2005): World Development Report 2006: Equity and Development, New York: Oxford University Press

Yat-Sen, Sun (1927): San Min Chu I, (Trans. Frank W Price), Shanghai: China Committee, Institute of Pacific Relations

Index

H

I

152, 154
structural adjustment
programmes. (See
Structural adjustment
programmes, and subject
countries)
International Union for Land Value
Taxation, The 175, 177
Investment. (See Capital,
investment of, and Private
investment, and Property
investment, and Public
investment)
Iron Curtain, The 23
Italy 77
Iyer, Lakshmi 31

J

Jacoby, Hanan 159
Jensen, Merrill 132
Jupp, Sir Kenneth 132–134
Justice. (See also Injustice)
in China 97
in South Africa 154
intergenerational 65, 68, 70, 134,
140
natural 67
post-colonial 107
principles of 10-12, 91, 175

K

Kalahari Bushmen 54, 57, 176
Kalahari Desert 53, 57, 176
Kiao Chan 96 (n. 9)
Killing poverty
the only way to 152, 164, 165.

192

(See also Social capitalism,
and Poverty, consigning to
history)
Klein, Naomi 12, 29 (n. 10)
Korea, South 173-174
Kuomintang 95, 97

L

Labour
cost of 101
forced 79, 83, 89
in India 94
returns to 60-61, 101-103, 116,
126, 145, 146. (See also
Wages)
taxation of 43, 129
Lancaster House Agreement 108.
(See also Zimbabwe)
Land
agricultural 9, 64, 69, 106
and crime levels 160
birthright in 8, 93, 124, 135, 174
charges on use of. (See Land,
taxation of)
common 32, 107, 109, 158. (See
also Commons, the, and
Community Land Trusts)
data on values of 89, 159
definition of 147 (n. 15)
distribution of 17, 77-79, 83, 89,
145-146, 156, 157, 173
enclosure 158 (n. 12)
grabs 9, 62, 77, 80 (n. 5), 97, 111,
113, 125, 145
historic process 67, 158 (n. 12)
idle 154
in Bolivia 83
in Botswana 52–54
in pre-colonial times 51

the IU

THE INTERNATIONAL UNION
FOR LAND VALUE TAXATION

The IU is an international umbrella organisation for land and tax reformers. It has members in 35 countries around the world—activists, politicians, professionals and academics, and over 70 national and local organisations. The IU's objective is "to stimulate in all countries a public opinion favourable to permanent peace and prosperity for all people, through the progressive removal of the basic economic causes of poverty and war". The IU engages in international initiatives in support of its objectives and enjoys Special Consultative Status at the United Nations.

www.theIU.org

FRED HARRISON is a graduate of the Universities of Oxford and London.

His journalistic career in Fleet Street was followed by a 10-year sojourn in Russia—where *inter alia* he was an adviser to the federal Parliament and to the Economics Department of the Russian Academy of Sciences.

He is Research Director of the London-based Land Research Trust, and co-founder of the communications company Motherlode Ltd and web-broadcaster The Renegade Economist.